COURAGE
TO CARE

Praise for *Courage to Care*

Stanley Hagemeyer has drawn on his extensive experience—as a pastor, teacher and trainer—to provide a practical guide for those who want to learn how to care for people who are suffering. I recommend *Courage to Care* as an important resource to pastors and laymen alike.

> —JARRETT RICHARDSON, MD, Psychiatrist and Hospice/Palliative Care Clinician, Rochester, Minnesota

Courage to Care is a must read for anyone who has ever felt pain or cared for someone who does—and that is everyone! I wish I had this book when I was in seminary, and I intend to make it known to the hundreds of seminary students I work with now! Stan Hagemeyer's wisdom is sage and his counsel is empowering.

> —DR. TIMOTHY BROWN, Henry Bast Professor of Preaching and President Emeritus, Western Theological Seminary, Holland, Michigan

Reverend Stan Hagemeyer has captured the essence of what it takes to reach out to the lost and broken people around us, which could actually be any of us. From his experience in ministry, combined with the stories of those who have discovered deep joy in giving care, this book is a treasure of insight, guidance and wisdom. In the words of Ezekiel 3:3, "Eat this scroll."

> —CRAIG SMITH, MS Clinical Psychology, Manistee, Michigan

Rev. Stanley Hagemeyer shares from years of experience as a pastor and caregiver and gives many examples of caregiving that benefit both the recipient and the giver. He shares how the relationship brings spiritual growth and fulfillment in the lives of caregivers and sufferers alike as they experience the manifest presence of Jesus and the working of the Holy Spirit in their interactions.

> —SHERRY HARTLEY, Director of Prayer, College of Prayer International, Lilburn, Georgia

Courage to Care is the kind of guidance we all so desperately need when those we know and love are facing life's biggest challenges. It answers the question of how we come alongside others in healthy and helpful ways, without being overwhelmed ourselves. I highly recommend this as a primary resource for both the individual and the congregational care team.

—KEITH J. FOISY, DMin, Ludington, Michigan

Stan Hagemeyer's book is excellent for those getting started with caregiving. I also found in it the *language* of caregiving that helps me express why I have found much joy and great reward in this practice for over forty years. It's a practice that finds both giver and receiver vulnerable, available, and in a position to find healing of all sorts. Read it, teach it, practice it, share it. You will thank Stan for being your guide.

—ROBERT BRAMAN, MDiv, PhD, Stanton, Michigan

In a world where so many feel disconnected from authentic community, this book offers a bridge to deep, intimate relationships that can sustain us through even the hardest times. I cannot recommend it more highly!

—REV. DR. DOUG RESLER, Parker Evangelical Presbyterian Church, Parker, Colorado

As a pastor, I'm always on the hunt for practical tools that will enable me to do ministry more effectively. *Courage to Care* provides not just one or two care-ministry tools but a whole toolbox full—complete with practical and biblical instructions. This is the work not of an academic ministry theoretician but of a caring pastor who's been in the trenches. I am a pastor today in large part because of the positive, caring example I saw in Stanley Hagemeyer. I'll be providing each member of my staff with their personal copy of this important book.

—JOHN A. HOUSTON, Lead Pastor, Point Harbor Church, Chesapeake, Virginia

COURAGE TO CARE

You Can Help Others Who Are Suffering

♥

STANLEY HAGEMEYER

Editor: Bob Hartig
Interior design: Beth Shagene
Cover design: Jeff Gifford

Dedicated to Roger and Marcia Weeks

Contents

Introduction

ONE OF MY GREAT JOYS OVER THE PAST TWO OR THREE DECADES IS seeing how lay people, ordinary people, can do great things in ministry. They come with their own compassion for others, and with a little training, they gain the confidence to go where people are in trouble, in pain, or suffering. Skills added to compassion have yielded great results.

There will never be enough clergy or counselors to take care of everyone who is hurting. I am convinced that the New Testament vision of ministry was the whole body of Christ caring for the whole circle of people among and around us. And it is not burdensome. Rather, this business of intersecting people's lives when they are hurting leads to real satisfaction and a godly joy that comes from sharing the journey of life with someone.

But there are a couple problems. For one, while training care teams in several churches, I have seen that people are often hesitant to go where they are most needed—where someone is in real pain or trouble. But suffering is ubiquitous. Everyone faces it at some time, and when we do, we need someone confident enough to be present and be an encouraging friend.

The other problem is that few resources are available to prepare us to go alongside those who are hurting. This book explains practices and attitudes that empower ordinary people to be effective caregivers who make a world of difference for people in trouble.

So why read this book? You will want to if you care about others who are hurting.

Do you know anyone who is in trouble?

Someone who is in pain, is grieving, or is afraid?

Anyone who is going through a crisis?

Perhaps your response is the same as mine earlier in my life: "Yes, but I have no idea what to do, so I avoid such situations."

What if you could see them as tremendous opportunities? You can learn how to really help others! You do not need to be a professional clergy person or a counselor. Anyone can learn to show caring support in ways that are very simple.

But first you need to get past your fears and hesitations. This book will build your courage to do that and go on to be an effective, caring friend.

───── ❤ ─────

You have had pain of your own, maybe more at times than most people experience. So why get involved in others' troubles? Here is why: In doing so, you will

- create connections with people you will never forget
- learn much from another's pain
- know times of deep joy
- fulfill your calling to bear one another's burdens
- experience deep satisfaction and meaning in life
- allow God to demonstrate his love to others through you

Those of us who want to help someone in distress—a family member, a friend, or anyone else—are called to a wonderful ministry. But it can create a rift in our emotions. We want to bring relief, to reduce that person's suffering. We long to help. Yet at the same time, we feel our own frustration, and we want to ease it. We want to get away, back to where the problem can be ignored, at least temporarily. We are torn between our care for another and our sense of inadequacy. This book will help you gain courage to overcome the fear of your own limitations. You will learn ways to live out the habits that show up in Jesus.

I will tell you about real people who faced the challenge and found ways to help that blessed both the sufferer and themselves. I interviewed dozens of people. Some were professionals, some were family members, some were lay people in roles of caregiving. Many of them told me of the satisfaction their encounters brought to them. Some spoke with profound feeling about their work and even described it with joy. In the most desperate situations it might seem unlikely that joy is anywhere on the horizon. But it surfaces again and again.

What Is in This Book?

Each chapter begins with a quick list of key points the chapter covers. From there, we'll unpack three kinds of information.

We'll look at Jesus's example and how his model points the way for us. This provides a biblical framework for the everyday things God calls us to do. Jesus loved people with a courageous, risky form of love. His ways of serving point to the ways we, as caregivers, can offer his love as well.

Second, we'll consider caregivers who have found ways that really made a difference. Some navigated their way through distress that could intimidate anyone. Some will shock you by their boldness in dangerous situations. You'll see people demonstrating courageous, risky, and profoundly unselfish love while serving people who are in real trouble.

Third, these studies demonstrate concrete actions, attitudes, and approaches that anyone can learn. These examples will stick in your mind and guide your own adventures in caring. Satisfaction and gratitude await you in ways you'd never expect. You'll find courage to care, perhaps through your church or other venue, and in all your daily encounters. And you will be inspired to bless your family and friends with your loving ways.

Who Is This Book For?

You may be a care team member or deacon. You are expected to visit the sick. Or you may simply want to help others. If you care about others, this book will give you confidence and practical examples of successful caring. Helping others who are hurting will take you on a journey of discovery. This approach can become a part of who you are and how you live.

If you know someone in pain and would like to help, this book is for you. If you are anxious about encountering other people's sadness, suffering, anger, or fear, this book is for you. I will show you how you can gain a harvest of unexpected blessings. This book will describe a bigger story, one you will want to be a part of. It will embolden you to be there for someone in time of suffering, because you have the courage to care.

For Clarification

The word *caregiver* in this book is used for anyone—whether a friend, a volunteer, or a professional—who is involved in caring for the needs of someone who is suffering or in difficult circumstances.

The stories in this book are true. Names of people, with few exceptions, have been changed to protect their privacy. Events and conversations are told as accurately as possible.

Appreciating Suffering

KEY POINTS IN THIS CHAPTER

1 Suffering and pain are present in the lives of people we see every day.

2 Learning about someone's suffering is an especially potent way to show love and respect.

3 People who tell their stories to an attentive listener feel appreciated and valued and are helped toward healing.

We are all experts on suffering. Each of us has experienced it in some way. Whether from an illness, a catastrophic injury, or disappointment in a relationship, we are each an expert in one area—our own pain.

More than likely, some event has burned its way into your memory so deeply that you can remember it like yesterday. It was intense. It was painful, perhaps humiliating, disappointing, or frustrating.

We've all been there. We are experts on the turmoil and discord pain brings. And yet . . .

We are all ignorant. When someone else tells us how much it hurts, we can listen and try to understand. But we don't really know what it feels like for that person to wake up at 2:00 a.m. and ponder the hopelessness of it all. The person's pain is their own; it cannot be adopted. We can only gather clues to what he or she is going through.

When lovers first develop a deep relationship, they tell one another all their hopes and dreams. They search for ways to share themselves. They delight in *knowing* one another.

Yet we live life as individuals—and while that is a good thing, it means there is always a gap in our ability to fully know another soul. When pain is prominent, that gap becomes critical. A friend may say, honestly, "I can't tell you how it feels." Or a husband or wife, desiring not to burden us, may out of love decide not to share the whole picture. We become "secondary sufferers," experiencing our own pain and confusion as we ponder that person's struggle. How can we respond in ways that will really help?

The calling of a Christian caregiver beckons us to bridge the chasm when pain on the other side is crying out like a voice in a storm.

❤

As a young man, I felt it important to tell people all about the things I had learned in my years of higher education. I thought that would help others know about God the way I did.

My youthful arrogance was slowly tempered as I began to intersect the lives of hurting people. Their stories began to educate me in a new way. Instead of telling them something that might help, I learned to listen.

That's the first thing we need to do if we really want to help: ask people to tell us more about their lives. When someone is having a difficult time, we need to listen before we talk much about ourselves and our own concerns. We need to open the gate with comments like "Tell me more about how that happened." Questions like "How does it feel to be in this situation?"

Don't be afraid you'll make the pain worse. You won't if you listen well. If you don't hurry to offer solutions. If you take time to simply be present.

I will provide tools to help you improve your listening skills later in this book. For now, it's important to realize that you don't need to become an expert. But you *can* become more effective as a compassionate friend when the other person realizes you appreciate their suffering.

To *appreciate* means giving value to something, raising its meaning in your life and valuing the person to whom you are listening. To appreciate someone's experience is to validate that person's right to feel the way they do about their story.

Appreciate suffering. It is a beginning.

Alberto

For several years I made a special effort to interview the older folks I met who were veterans of World War II. For me it was a way of learning history from those who had lived it. I enjoyed the modest way they shared stories of their perils, their victories, their coming of age in wartime. Almost all of them were teenagers when they entered military service. I found them fascinating, and I realized they felt some satisfaction in sharing their stories of both mundane events and the wildest adventures. One man in particular struck me deeply.

Alberto was a diminutive gentleman whom I met at a garage while waiting for my car repairs to be finished. He was quiet-spoken, dressed in work clothes, and I learned that he occasionally ran errands for the garage. Having recognized his age, one day I asked him if he had served in the military. Yes, he had been a flight engineer on a bomber crew in World War II. That piqued my interest. We talked for a while. The next time I saw him I asked if he was willing to meet with me sometime when he could tell me his whole story. He reluctantly agreed. We met a few days later at a quiet place where there would be no interruptions. With a little prompting from me, he unfolded his story.

Alberto had grown up in New Mexico and was of Hispanic descent. After volunteering to join the Army Air Corps, he was pleased to be given the education and opportunity to become a flight engineer on a B-24 crew. I asked him what that position meant. He explained that the flight engineer was a qualified airplane mechanic who did the final inspection before every takeoff. Then during flight he monitored the plane's operation, and if a mechanical failure occurred or enemy fire damaged critical components, he would scramble to make a fix while in the air. He also functioned as the top turret gunner. I was impressed that there was more to this quiet little guy than I had thought.

Making bombing runs over Europe was a harrowing experience. The planes were shot at by enemy fighters, and antiaircraft shells saturated the air near the targets. The crews usually returned from every mission with holes in their aircraft. Alberto told of his anguish at seeing a friend's plane disintegrate in the sky. And he felt a confusing sorrow as his own plane's bombs fell successfully, because he knew they were killing ordinary people caught up in a war they could not escape.

Every trip was a test of survival and wits. And then the time came when Alberto and his crewmates did not return. On his tenth mission, their plane was hit over enemy territory and severely damaged, with only one engine still running. The captain ordered them to abandon ship. Crew members lined up at a door to parachute out. In those terrifying moments the man just ahead of him froze at the door. Alberto yelled at him again and again to jump! Jump! In the noise and the wild gushing air, he did not move. Finally Alberto gave him a push. The man flew out into the air, but he did not open his chute, and his safety cord had not been hooked inside the plane to automatically open it.

Alberto himself jumped quickly and opened his own chute, but he watched his crewmate plunge to his death. Alberto was tormented for a long time after, wondering if he was responsible. Yet he had done the only thing he could.

He was captured and spent eight months in various German POW camps. How Alberto survived is a story in itself. Eventually the war ended, and like many airmen, he was rescued and returned home. His face lit up with a special smile as he told how his father, upon hearing the news that Alberto had landed in New York and was on his way home, was so grateful he rode his horse thirty miles to the church in Santa Fe to pray and give thanks to God. "They were so glad I had made it through."

It was a wonderful conclusion to a harrowing story, and I thanked Alberto for taking the time to tell me so much. But then he looked at me quizzically. "Do you know what is the worst part of all this?" he said.

I replied that I could not guess. He said, "My son doesn't know about these things. Whenever I have started to tell him a little about my time in the service, he says he doesn't want to hear about all that old stuff. He doesn't care about it at all. That's what is the worst of it all. Nobody has heard my whole story until you asked me to tell you about it."

I sat there in silence for a moment. I felt what a privilege it was to hear this gentle, humble man's story about some of the most exciting, terrifying, and painful experiences of his young life. And I was dumbfounded that his family, his own son, had not wanted to know. When I said so, Alberto sighed deeply. I sensed the deep pain that had weighed on him heavily over the years.

I had entered the conversation expecting an account of one man's personal adventure and sacrifice in the war. But I encountered more than I expected. I had not intended to make a caring visit to help bring some hope and healing to a person in pain. But after many years, Alberto had found someone genuinely interested in hearing his memories of danger and fear amidst combat, and the searing moment as he gazed at his crewmate falling to his death. He had told me about being locked in a POW compound, unsure of the future and out of touch for months and months. Alberto had experienced more pain and loss than most of us who have not known combat will ever know. But the quiet ache in his heart as a father seemed the deepest wound of all.

He thanked me for listening, and I assured him I was grateful for his sharing so much with me.

What went on that day? Alberto learned that I valued his suffering the pains and terrors of war. That I felt for his sadness as a father missing the connection with his son, a very special kind of suffering. As a man and as a father, Alberto felt appreciated through our conversation. Our time together affirmed the importance of the life he shared with me. He felt valued.

Appreciating Makes a Difference

When we value the experience of a person who is hurting, that is what it means to appreciate suffering. When we pay attention, we communicate value. We are saying, "You are important enough for me to pay attention to you. You are important enough to care about and spend time getting to know you."

People often tried to shield Jesus from those who wanted his attention. But no one was unimportant to him, as this little episode shows:

> As Jesus approached Jericho, a blind man was sitting by the road-side begging. When he heard the crowd going by, he asked what was happening. They told him, "Jesus of Nazareth is passing by."
>
> He called out, "Jesus, Son of David, have mercy on me!"
>
> Those who led the way rebuked him and told him to be quiet, but he shouted all the more, "Son of David, have mercy on me!"
>
> Jesus stopped and ordered the man to be brought to him. When he came near, Jesus asked him, "What do you want me to do for you?"
>
> "Lord, I want to see," he replied.
>
> Jesus said to him, "Receive your sight; your faith has healed you." Immediately he received his sight and followed Jesus, praising God. When all the people saw it, they also praised God. (Luke 18:35–43)

Like the blind man, there are often hurting people around us whom we could easily overlook. My conversation with Alberto put me in touch with a man's unexpected need, and caregiving resulted. Spontaneous opportunities can happen for you too if you watch for them.

Remarkable encounters can occur when we visit someone who is troubled. When we wait at the side of someone in pain. When we listen carefully. When we ask someone how they really are and invite them to tell us more. Our attitude of appreciation will communicate the love of God in crucial moments.

Do not hesitate to appreciate the presence of suffering. It can be a doorway to a deeper relationship and to healing and hope.

Alberto illustrates that suffering comes in many forms. It may be purely physical pain. It may be fear and apprehension of what will happen next. It may be loneliness or grief for what has been lost or never gained, a hope extinguished. Alberto reminded me to pay attention to older people in my family or community, to encourage them to share their stories before it is too late.

This encounter reminded me how important it is to listen well. We don't want to miss out on learning great lessons or enjoying the adventures of someone's life that lie dormant behind a wrinkled smile, waiting to be shared if only we pay attention.*

The more we understand other people's suffering and the emotions that attend it, the likelier we are to manage our own emotions and listen intelligently. When we dare to engage with hurting people, we will learn more about suffering and about ourselves as well. Each step brings us closer to the cross and to the joy that Jesus saw in that cross.

> Let us fix our eyes on Jesus, the author and perfecter of our faith, who for the joy set before him endured the cross, scorning its shame. (Hebrews 12:2 NIV 1984)

Conclusion

If we pay attention, we will often discover people with a story to tell, a story that includes suffering. Such occasions are opportunities rich with possibility. By listening well, we can be of help to another person and learn valuable life lessons as well.

---

*Resources and exercises to improve your listening skills and build your confidence can be found in appendix A

FOR DISCUSSION OR PERSONAL REFLECTION

1 People experience suffering in several forms: physical, emotional, relational, spiritual. Which have you experienced? Which has touched you most deeply?

2 How do you feel when someone listens well as you describe your own tough times?

3 What is one thing you learned from someone who told you about their experience of suffering?

CHAPTER 2

Crossing into Alien Territory

KEY POINTS IN THIS CHAPTER

1 Effective caregivers overcome their fears and enter into uncomfortable places to be with people in trouble.

2 Taking the to be with someone in trouble allows us to share their burdens and pain.

3 The sense of risk we take can bring feelings of confusion and a challenge to our identity.

4 Preparing for the challenge involves study, prayer, and consulting with supportive friends.

PAIN IS AN UNWELCOME GUEST. WE PREFER TO AVOID IT IF AT ALL possible. We want to get away from our own pain or have it treated. And most of us also find it disconcerting to be in the presence of someone who is suffering in some way. Pain is like an alien force with the power to distort all our thoughts and feelings. In order to be present for a sufferer, we have to struggle with our own aversion to their pain on the one hand, and on the other hand, with our compassion and desire to help them.

So we have a problem: How do we manage our repulsion and discomfort when we feel called alongside someone who hurts? This chapter considers that challenge in a way that will motivate and equip you to follow Jesus's pattern of caring.

Mike Yankoski and Sam Purvis spent five months in five different cities living as homeless people. They wanted to learn firsthand what it is like to be homeless. Much of what they learned was disturbing. In his journal, Yankoski describes an occasion where they were sitting in a coffee shop. In a nearby corner a group of people, evidently Christians, was discussing the Bible. "As they walked past us" when the group broke up, wrote Yankoski, "Sam and I looked up, trying to catch their eyes and nod a hello. But they carefully looked away. Each emptied their tray of garbage into the trash can next to Sam and turned to walk down the stairs."[1] He speculates that his and Sam's odor might have had something to do with this avoidance. They had not bathed for three or four weeks. But that excuse did not lessen the pain of being so clearly ignored. They felt devalued. They were "not seen" because they were invisible nonpersons to the passing Christians. Evidently, those who walked by so quickly did not handle their own discomfort well and could not bridge the gap to say hello.

We may not encounter bad odors when we try to help someone in need—or we may. So what? Tony Campolo tells of buying an extra take-out cup of coffee for a homeless man. The man was overcome with gratitude. With the crumbs of his last meal clinging to his mangy beard, he reached out to hug Tony. Campolo describes his own conflicting emotions. Although repulsed by the smells, the dirt, and the possibility of disease, he also felt the love of Christ as the unwashed gentleman ardently expressed his gratitude for the coffee and his affection for Tony.[2] Likewise, we need to pay attention to our gut reactions and recognize when our feelings create an invisible wall. With the love of Christ and a compelling motivation to love our neighbor, we can overcome our fears in order to be near those who suffer.

Family or friends sometimes also feel confused or conflicted, and they let their emotions steer them away. For example, they may make only short, symbolic visits and quickly leave to get away from their inner distress. Their inattentiveness can add to the pain of the sufferer. Their unwillingness to talk about what is really happening to a dying person will leave a sense of disconnect instead of bringing deeper friendship and care. When the physician has said, "I'm afraid your chances are not very good," someone with this dismal prognosis experiences an added dimension of alienation if people seem to distance themselves. It's easy for the patient to conclude, "Nobody really understands. Perhaps nobody even really cares."

Mother Teresa has so aptly pointed out that the primary form of suffering in the Western world is not physical illness but, rather, a deep and pervading loneliness that affects people of all social levels.[3]

But sometimes someone who loves them deeply will reach across the barrier and stay near through the agonizing hours.

How are we to get up the inclination to go where the pain is? How do we gain the courage to go where suffering is consuming the joys of life for someone—the courage to care?

Overcoming Our Fears

Once we recognize the nature of our own fears, we can take steps to get past them. Are we ready to accept that doing what God calls us to do—offer our time and attention to a person who is at their worst—could be painful? Fear and anxiety cloud our vision and confuse our thinking, and excuses to delay or avoid the visit easily arise.

But such challenges are normal. Doctors, nurses, clergy, and volunteer caregivers deal with them successfully every day. They have learned to manage their inner reactions and focus instead on the needs of the patient. Some family members show wonderfully effective love. Still, for a lot of us, caregiving is akin to stepping into alien territory, like crossing a divide into a threatening landscape.

Can you see yourself as a daring explorer? An explorer prepares for the difficult journey ahead. If we will take this approach, we can gain the courage and motivation to overcome our resistance. We can instead deliberately seek opportunities to be with those bearing physical pain and emotional suffering. One way to gain confidence when we are traveling is to learn about the territory ahead and recognize when we are crossing into that unfamiliar zone. We may not know the exact path, but there are signs along the way that indicate we are moving in the right direction.

Crossing Boundaries

When we enter a place where someone is suffering, we are temporarily leaving behind our own well-being, our own comfort, our own health, to be near that person's world of discomfort. We cannot know what it really feels like for them. If we have had cancer and are visiting a cancer patient, we may remember our own feelings during that episode in our lives. If we have been divorced, we will have insights to guide us when visiting a separated or divorced person. But their world is still not ours; it is a foreign country. So let's consider a fresh perspective on that boundary crossing.

Jesus invitation to "come, follow me" (Mark 1:17) is familiar to most of us as Christians. But it still ought to provoke some curiosity or mystery. Follow him where? Where did Jesus go? He tells us: "Whoever wants to be my disciple must deny themselves and take up their cross and follow me" (Mark 8:34). This is a call to much more than a private walk in the garden with Jesus. It could involve everything from cultivating a special relationship with our next-door neighbors or serving the homeless to doing missionary work in some faraway place fraught with dangers.

Most of the time, a cross and martyrdom are remote, though life-and-death challenges do exist. Jesus's followers die every day somewhere in the world. But what else could it mean to follow Jesus and carry a cross?

Pain is everywhere if we look for it. Disappointment, worry, and fear are a part of life we all share. Jesus challenges us to explore suffering by heeding his call and following his pattern.

With that in mind, let's reconsider his words "Come, follow me." Could he be calling us to do as he did—to deliberately enter a world of sin and suffering, to come right into the danger zone? To overcome our reluctance and cross a boundary into the alien world of another person's pain?

Kristin

Kristin is a nurse whose level of competence, education, and experience made her a high-level administrator in a large hospital. She had the respect of her peers. She knew she did good work. But somehow she had grown to feel unfulfilled.

So she began looking for a different, more engaging way of bringing medical care to people in need. As a single person, she could move freely. And after a while she found a new challenge, which has turned out to be a long-term adventure.

When I visited Kristin, she had been pursuing her adventure for five years. She worked in a thirty-four-bed facility in Washington, DC, that cares for only one kind of patient: homeless men who have been hospitalized but need convalescent care after being discharged. The facility is run purely on grace, since there are no paying customers, other than those who have Medicaid or VA health-care benefits. Were it not for this facility, these patients would be back on the street at an extremely vulnerable time in their recovery. Many have chronic health problems. Some are addicted to alcohol or have drug dependency problems. Many have had repulsive lifestyles.

Yet Kristin described her life to me with exuberance. She finds real joy and fulfillment in this work. She has seen a few lives change permanently for good.

Certainly not all, though. Kristin works in an unattractive neighborhood among people whom many of us would tend to avoid. Some men return more than once. But her patients love her tender, caring attitude. And she says, "In five years here, I have never awakened in the morning and felt I did not want to go to work!" She is happy.

Kristin is a living example of the incarnation of God's love. She heard Jesus's call, "Follow me," and she is one of the happiest people I have ever met. Her joy becomes a gift to the men she sees every day.

Certainly there is a cross in this picture. There is a cost.

But there is also love, and there is joy.

People such as Kristin are inspiring in their self-sacrifice. We hear such stories from time to time, and most of us marvel at them. Why? Because someone has gone beyond the norm, beyond what is easy and familiar. They dared to go into alien territory. They crossed the boundary into another person's world and embraced discomfort they could have avoided.

Boundaries come in a multitude of forms. As a pastor, I will never forget the first time I entered the home of a family where someone had committed suicide. I did not want to go. I felt inadequate. I was unsure of what to say or do. I was afraid of the pain. But I was called.

We can each name circumstances we'd prefer to avoid, but we know someone should be there. Grave illness. Disability. Marriage discord or family abuse. Unemployment, alcoholism, moral failure, criminal court, teenage pregnancy, drug abuse, the death of a spouse . . . Your list may include some I have overlooked. The boundaries we are called to cross differ depending on who we are and what situation we face. But in every case, feelings of fear and inadequacy will threaten our discipleship.

We need to look to Jesus for the courage and understanding we need. We want to be known as his followers, his brothers and sisters. Paul tells us this will include both welcome and unwelcome elements. "We are . . . co-heirs with Christ, if indeed we share in his sufferings in order that we may also share in his glory" (Romans 8:17).

Life has all kinds of ways to undo a person's sense of value and stability. Those who reach out to others in a caring way are precious friends. And it is often the most ordinary of people who practice extraordinary love by crossing such boundaries. Two such people were Frank and Eileen.

Frank and Eileen

When Frank and Eileen's pastor and his wife separated, everyone in their church was disturbed by this turn of events. The pastor continued in most of his normal roles, leading worship, visiting with the sick or shut-ins. But a gray cloud traveled around with him. He felt like he was fulfilling a role in a play.

Most members of the flock hoped their pastoral couple would get over it soon and everyone could get back to "normal life." A few attempted to share their well-intentioned advice, but it was not very helpful.

Like so many separated but not yet divorced persons, the pastor and his wife each felt isolated. The pastor said it was like a moat around a castle. She began attending a different church but returned occasionally for some special event like a baptism.

Some people said they just didn't want to get involved—the situation was too uncomfortable. A few visited one or the other spouse. On Thanksgiving weekend the wife traveled to another state with their two children to visit her family. A couple from the pastor's flock invited him to come to their own family dinner, offering him relief during what could have been a long, lonely holiday.

But Frank and Eileen went a lot farther. On his lunch break, Frank would often call the pastor and invite him for a bite to eat. Previously, Frank had only a passing acquaintance with his minister, but now he took steps to make it more personal. Frank had no agenda except to offer friendly companionship, and the pastor responded with appreciation.

Then Frank and Eileen took another step. On the alternating weekends when the pastor had his two young boys with him, he had to return them to their mother Sunday evening. During those first few weeks, that handoff time was an emotionally draining experience. But soon after the young pastor returned to his nondescript upper-story apartment, he got a phone call. It was Frank, asking if he would like to come over for popcorn and a TV show Frank liked. Who could refuse this innocent pleasure?

This led to a pattern of involvement and steadily deepening relationships. Frank and Eileen were cheerful people who made the pastor comfortable, and their attitude encouraged him to just be himself. After a few weeks they gently inquired about his experience with the separation and listened without offering advice or judgment. They became his fast friends. Their own teenagers popped in from time to time, and their family presence was a healing power that warmed the pastor's life. They made him feel normal. They clearly enjoyed his presence, and cheerful banter was as common as deeper conversations. He felt cared for, welcomed, and healthy.

Opening up still more, the pastor shared that preparing sermons was now much harder. He often doubted his own judgment whether his ideas were worthwhile or well expressed. His insecurity led him to write out manuscripts rather than speak extemporaneously from an outline, as he had always done. Eileen offered to read his message early in the week and listen to him explain it. She became his partner in sermon preparation, offering comments and suggestions. Most of these were affirming, but her questions for clarification also helped him sharpen his expression.

This unique couple made a big difference in helping their pastor through a rough year. At the same time, they were doing another caring ministry parallel to his and unknown to him. On the Friday nights when he took custody of his boys at 6:00 p.m., his wife usually remained home to struggle with her own sense of loss after the boys went out the front door. Soon after the separation, she began receiving her own Friday evening phone calls from Eileen, asking whether she would like to come over for dessert or go out shopping. The mom who was missing her children was invited into Frank and Eileen's family, enjoying the same cheerful atmosphere her husband did on Sunday evenings. Again the lighthearted banter and obvious care led to a deepening relationship. She enjoyed these new friends who helped make life bearable again.

Frank and Eileen knew how to cross boundaries in order to offer unconditional love. While others hesitated, this couple showed they cared deeply and went out of their way to help. They offered very little advice, and then only when it was requested. They were practical. They were good listeners. They kept confidences. *And they were not professionals.* Frank did not have even a high school diploma. He was a warehouse foreman and successful at his work. Eileen was employed part-time as a beautician. But they knew how to care for the hurting. They innately knew how to reach across the barriers that threatened to isolate the pastor and his wife. Where others hesitated, they went ahead because their compassion gave them courage to care.

Frank and Eileen demonstrated that reaching people who hurt takes a conscious effort. They took the initiative, and they persisted for weeks and months in a gentle intervention with a couple they hardly knew, showing reliable, unconditional love in action.

I know their story so well because it is mine as well. I am the pastor who was so blessed by this remarkable pair of disciples who went the whole distance with my wife and me.

Taking Initiative

One woman told me about her experience with an inept pastor and the ordinary form in which real help came to her. She had given birth to a severely disabled, malformed child. Her clergyman visited her just once in the hospital—briefly. Upon seeing the child, he stammered, "I've got to go—I'll be back." But he never returned, though she remained hospitalized for days. She was discharged from the hospital feeling ill prepared to actually care for her special-needs child while she still needed time for her own recovery. But that same day an older woman from her parish stopped by near the dinner hour with a casserole and a dessert. She knew meal time would create extra stress. She had little to say, but the young mother said, "I felt so relieved and grateful for that simple act of caring. She was a messenger from God."

We may have opportunity to join someone in a circumstance where we are both in foreign territory—court, for example. The offense may be as simple as a low-level misdemeanor or as serious and life-changing as a felony charge. Regardless, the courtroom can be a frightening and lonely place for the offender. An attorney may be present and helpful, but a friend who chooses to sit with the defendant makes a powerful statement of caring love.

I once arrived at a hospital to pray with a woman who was about to enter surgery. I was almost too late—she was already on a gurney, being wheeled down the hallway to the operating suite. I felt I had failed. But they stopped when she recognized me, and we prayed as the attendants waited. Later she told me that she felt it was exactly the right moment.

The further we extend ourselves into the arena of crisis, the more effective our efforts will be. Both we and the recipient of our care may be in foreign, unsettling territory, but we will be there together. And that is exactly where such contact will be most appreciated. We need to be present in that alien zone.

The effective caregiver takes the initiative. We don't wait for the hurting person to come to us—we make the contact, place the call, go to the person. Doing so declares powerfully our decision to be present in the other person's world—their home, their streets, their circumstances. That is exactly what Kristin chose to do when she left her comfortable hospital career to work in the inner city. It is what the woman with the casserole chose to do when she went to a house where there was pain and weariness.

We refer to Jesus's coming as a human being as his *incarnation*. The word literally means "in the flesh." Our own service to others is best when it is incarnational. A hurting person needs a friend who is present in the flesh.

Sam and LeRoy

Sam was a graduate student when he came down with mononucleosis. The doctors said it could be treated at home, but Sam had to be quarantined. No visitors allowed. Only his wife could come and go as usual. The physician recommended six weeks to make sure the contagion would be gone completely.

The first two weeks went by as expected. Sam tried to read the material for classes he was missing. But he tired easily and had to rest in bed much of the time. He watched TV for hours. The next two weeks dragged by. He felt better but found it difficult to put energy into studying. He saw no one for hours on end as his wife continued to go to work daily.

Then one day came a knock on the door. Sam's wife answered, and pretty soon Sam saw his fellow-student and friend, LeRoy, standing at the foot of the bed. "How are you, anyway, Sam?"

LeRoy's friendly voice filled the void. They talked for a few minutes. LeRoy said, "I know you're supposed to be isolated, but I just couldn't stay away any longer. I had to see you. I'm glad you're doing well." He soon left. But his presence made all the difference. Sam says he never forgot that moment. LeRoy had dared to cross the boundary. He was present in the flesh.

Phone calls, email, and social media can be helpful. But such brief contacts are too ephemeral. It is crucial for the hurting person to know we are in touch in a very real way. Incarnational ministry requires that we do our best to get close to someone. Being physically present gives us the best chance to really make a difference.

Following Jesus's Bold Example

A few key events in Jesus's life point to his total immersion in his place of ministry, the human race. Let's consider how complete was his transition to humanity.

First, look at how God arranged Jesus's crossing of boundaries. He was born to an obscure peasant girl in a makeshift accommodation (Luke 2). Joseph, who became her husband, was afflicted with doubts and confusion, just as her family and neighbors were uncertain of the baby's parentage. Christ became "God with us" (Emmanuel) in the most ordinary of ways. There is little recorded of his early years. But we do know he was trained as a skilled tradesman in a small town.

In one of his first notable public appearances, he insisted on entering the water to be baptized by his cousin, John (Matthew 3:13–17).

To all who were looking on, it would appear that he was just another repentant human being seeking forgiveness for his sins. When John objected, Jesus said simply, "Let it be so now."

In another of his early public encounters, he appeared in the synagogue in Nazareth, his hometown, where his childhood was well known.

> On the sabbath he began to teach in the synagogue, and many who heard him were astounded. They said, "Where did this man get all this? What is this wisdom that has been given to him? What deeds of power are being done by his hands! Is not this the carpenter, the son of Mary and brother of James and Joses and Judas and Simon, and are not his sisters here with us?" And they took offense at him. (Mark 6:2–3 NRSV)

He succeeded so well at being just an ordinary person in Nazareth that when he did begin to gain some notoriety, the people of his hometown couldn't believe it. "Isn't this the carpenter?"

Fast-forward to Gethsemane. Jesus, moved with emotion as he contemplated his own death, asked God that the cup of suffering be taken from him (Mark 14:33–36). It was a purely human reaction, showing how successfully he entered the human race. It was even necessary for Judas to plant a kiss on Jesus so the temple guard would know which of the men to arrest (v. 44). Surely no one has been more human.

Jesus crossed all the boundaries, a full incarnation of the Son of God into the human race. His example teaches us several things we can expect to experience when we too cross into alien territory.

Signs of Being in the Zone

"The Word became flesh" (John 1:14). That's why Jesus was so believable. And if we want to help another person, we too need to cross over in the flesh in some way and be in his or her world. That is incarnational ministry.

What are some signs of it? When do you know you are in the zone?

There are three indicators.

1. A Sense of Risk

When we cross into strange and unfamiliar territory, the first thing we may sense is the risk involved. Entering a hospital room, we wonder, *Should I be here?* Can we make any difference to the ill person?

Or perhaps we enter into conversation with someone heading for a divorce. Will our intentions be misunderstood? We may be perceived as taking sides. No matter how well we guard our judgment, we may be drawn into a view distorted by that person's lens. We will not have the whole picture.

Risk means that we engage in an action or endeavor without knowing how it will turn out. Risk comes with doing any kind of good. Showing compassion toward a person of the opposite sex creates the risk of being misunderstood or of inadvertently forming an unhealthy relationship. Helping someone get groceries one week may lead to their expecting our help the next week as well. We may be taken for granted. But compassionate caring does not allow us to avoid all risks. In fact, life amounts to nothing without taking risks. We can take preemptive steps to avoid being misunderstood. We can guard our thoughts. We can explain our motives, hopes, and intentions clearly. But we'll never fully eliminate risk.

Jesus took risks of all kinds. He risked the disapproval of his kinsmen in Nazareth. He risked talking with a Samaritan woman. He risked touching the leper. He risked the wrath of the establishment by challenging their authority. If we take risks for the right reasons, on behalf of his purposes, we are in good company.

2. Confusion

The more complicated a situation is, the more choices we have and the likelier we'll be confused about how best to help. For instance, someone who is out of work may just need our encouragement and affirmation. Passing on information about job openings *might* be helpful. But if that person is already searching diligently, such help may seem condescending.

Sitting next to someone in court during their arraignment can trigger another kind of confusion. What do others think of our association with that person? How do *we* feel about it, and why?

The point is, confusion and crossing boundaries often go hand in hand. We may even feel pain that is not our own. And those we are trying to help may misunderstand or disregard our attempts to help. Stretched way beyond our competence and comfort, we cry out, "Why, Lord?" In that moment, it's important to remember that our inner conflict mirrors the crisis the sufferer is experiencing.

Jesus endured the confusion of others more than he experienced his own confusion. People doubted his qualifications and his motives again and again. Remember the people's reaction to him in the synagogue of his own hometown, Nazareth? "Where did this man get all this? What is this wisdom that has been given to him?" (Mark 6:2 NRSV).

The Jerusalem leaders didn't even bother to wonder—they jumped straight to accusation: "He has Beelzebul, and by the ruler of the demons he casts out demons" (Mark 3:22 NRSV).

Even Jesus's own family thought he was crazy. "When his family heard it, they went out to restrain him, for people were saying, 'He has gone out of his mind'" (Mark 3:21 NRSV). How painful that must have been for Jesus!

But worst of all was that terrible moment of confusion for Jesus himself on the cross: "My God, my God, why have you forsaken me?" (Matthew 27:46).

When we endure confusion because we are out on a limb in our efforts to serve a hurting soul, we can take comfort in knowing we are in the very best of company—*his* company.

3. Our Identity Challenged

When we leave our comfort zone and step into someone else's experience, it's natural to do some soul searching. Who are we to think we can make a difference in that person's situation?

That question may be mirrored in the faces of doctors, attorneys, or other specialists. They may even ask, "Who are you?" or "What are you doing here?" It's important to clarify in our own minds our real purpose for being present.

We can risk our identity by simply being near someone in trouble. Not long ago I was waiting in the hallway outside a courtroom with an acquaintance who was involved in a marital dispute. I was there to give him moral support. While we waited in the outer hallway, the uniformed bailiff checked us over with a metal detector. I was dressed casually while my friend was dressed in a sharp business suite and carried a briefcase. Unaware why we were there, he chatted with us amiably, and it soon became clear from his remarks that he thought I was an offender and my friend was my attorney. My friend quickly explained, "No, I'm not an attorney. And he's not in trouble."

It was a humorous moment and we all chuckled. Still, I felt a brief discomfort to think I'd been seen as an offender waiting to appear in criminal court.

But a challenged identity can also be vital in our walk with God. In his lucid discussion of the Trinity, Arthur McGill writes, "If a man shares in the life of God, his real life will be found in the act of offering himself . . . in obedience to God, through service to his neighbors. The cross demonstrates that such offering involves a real letting-go of the self. It involves dispossession, loss of identity."

McGill concludes, "Every act of loving thrusts a person into this crisis of identity, and there is no escape from this peculiar kind of tension."[4]

Just as Jesus was misunderstood, we too will often be at risk when we seek to be present in the suffering of others. It is as though we are entering a twilight zone where people view things through a foggy lens. Our efforts will not always be viewed in the best light.

Preparing for the Challenge

How can we prepare for risk, confusion, and identity crisis? First, we need to focus our minds on the bigger picture. We are bringing light into a place where darkness threatens. "You are the light of the world," Jesus said (Matthew 5:14). And when we think, "No! I'm not up to that role," let's remember he made the same claim of himself: "I am the light of the world. Whoever follows me will never walk in darkness, but will have the light of life" (John 8:12).

We are meant to embody God's presence and communicate his love. So we can remind ourselves of our calling, as the people of God, to "bear one another's burdens, and so fulfill the law of Christ" (Galatians 6:2 RSV).

It is important that we prepare ourselves with prayer and meditation shaped by such texts. Reading certain Scripture passages reminds us who we are in Christ. For instance, Paul writes, "The Spirit himself testifies with our spirit that we are God's children" (Romans 8:16). Again, "We are therefore Christ's ambassadors, as though God were making his appeal through us" (2 Corinthians 5:20). Reading your favorite Scriptures that affirm your purpose can clear your mind.

We are best prepared also if we pray for the person we are about to see, and then pray for ourselves to be clearheaded and focused on our purpose of showing God's love rather than thinking about ourselves, our skills, and our inadequacies.

In caregiving, we will always benefit from being in a group of colleagues or even an informal circle of supportive friends who understand what we are trying to do. Such a circle can help us gain perspective and do a reality check about any concerns. Discussing our hopes and fears about particular situations can equip us for whatever challenges are involved. Preparing mentally and spiritually helps us experience greater calm.*

A psychologist friend of mine puts it this way: Feelings are contagious. When we are in someone's presence who is feeling depressed, lonely, angry, or afraid, we feel their darkness. But if we are prepared, centered on God's love working through us, we can be calm and accepting of whatever they feel and express. Then our own calm and peace are communicated to that needy person, offering them comfort, clarity of mind, and peace. God gives us positive feelings, and those feelings are contagious, too.

Something wonderful may happen inside us. When our sense of identity totters, amid the feelings of risk and confusion, we may gain a clearer grasp of our true identity in Christ. When we sense that we are doing what Christ Jesus wants us to be doing in a situation, we see ourselves in a new light. "Now you are the body of Christ, and each one of you is a part of it" (1 Corinthians 12:27). Living in his will and showing his love to others, we reflect him. "And we, who . . . reflect the Lord's glory, are being transformed into his likeness with ever-increasing glory, which comes from the Lord." (2 Corinthians 3:18 NIV 1984).

Why Bother?

If our attempts to do some good and be a caring person can cause so much trouble for us, why bother? Our answer will depend on our calling and our faith. But if we are intent on being disciples who seek to follow Jesus, we have potent reasons. We shouldn't expect a path of discipleship that costs nothing; if it does, we're on the wrong path. Jesus's path leads us to a deeper life rich with relationships and purpose. Being a Jesus follower draws us into all sorts of adventures. When we show love to people, we are following his pattern.

---

*For further help preparing for difficult challenges, see appendix D, "Nurturing the Caregiver."

Some of us are called to a uniquely challenging role when society takes a wrong turn. In Hitler's Germany, the nation's identity was utterly distorted and its governmental power usurped by evil. Dietrich Bonhoeffer, a bright young professor of theology in Germany, was deeply troubled by the Nazi government's domination of the Christian churches.

He accepted an invitation to be a visiting lecturer in New York and arrived in June 1939. But he soon wondered if he should have come. Several colleagues invited him to stay in the United States to avoid Nazi oppression in his home country. But Bonhoeffer wrote to his friend Reinhold Niebuhr in July of that year, "I have come to the conclusion that I have made a mistake in coming to America. I must live through this difficult period of our national history with the Christian people of Germany. I will have no right to participate in the reconstruction of Christian life in Germany after the war if I do not share the trials of this time with my people."[5]

Bonhoeffer returned home to help lead the resistance against Hitler's grip on the church. He organized and taught in an illegal underground seminary, encouraged courageous discipleship in others, and eventually became involved in a plot to assassinate Hitler. Arrested and imprisoned for three years, he ministered to his fellow prisoners, with whom he shared an uncertain fate. In April 1945, as Allied armies were drawing near, he was executed.

Dietrich Bonhoeffer "knew that true Christian worship and spirituality . . . [must] drive the Christian into the world's suffering and pain."[6] We may not encounter as much danger and loss as Bonhoeffer, but I hope his example will inspire you take risks that are uniquely yours in order to bring Christ's love to people who need its touch.

Conclusion

Being effective caregivers requires us to dare to go places we might normally never go and to be with people in times of trial and trouble. Such challenges will rattle our own security and confidence, but they will yield the harvest of greatly helping someone in need. If we prepare for these opportunities, we will experience life and healing from the Lord, who is working through us.

The next chapter shows how God's simple gifts in us can be potent tools to overcome the sufferer's distressing barriers.

FOR DISCUSSION OR PERSONAL REFLECTION

1 If you have been near someone who is suffering, what were some of your own feelings at that time? Why did you feel that way?

2 What kind of situation (e.g., a hospital, a prison, a person in hospice, someone going through divorce) would be alien territory for you? Name a type of suffering or a place you wish to avoid.

3 If you have risked being with someone in trouble, what resulted from that experience?

4 Think of a time when you felt God's call to follow him into a troubled circumstance. How did you experience him calling you?

CHAPTER 3

Simple Gifts
Make the Difference

KEY POINTS IN THIS CHAPTER

1 Sufferers experience things that tend to cut them off from others and hinder their healing. Some of these are:

> Feeling like an object
>
> Losing control of your Life
>
> Isolation and loneliness
>
> Alienation in marital breakdown
>
> Loneliness at the end of life

2 Caregivers can help people surmount such barriers by following Jesus's model of caring behavior:

> Tender touch
>
> Conversation that connects
>
> Daring presence with the lowly
>
> Daring to be vulnerable
>
> Going all the way to the edge

We have been looking at crossing bounds into someone's life from the side of the caregiver. Now let's look at it from the sufferer's point of view. We'll use the term *barrier* as we examine some of the feelings and perceptions that can cut off a hurting person from other people.

The deeply distressful situations that occur in every family or faith community easily lead to isolation. Barriers rise in response to all kinds of circumstances—a medical condition, a relationship breakdown, a financial setback, bankruptcy, unemployment, even a temporary illness. A person in such situations often feels disconnected from the world everyone else is living in.

The way friends, medical staff, and clergy treat a hurting person can also create barriers. Ill-conceived interactions, though well intentioned, frequently make the person feel all the more isolated and lonely, hopeless of ever getting any real help. He or she may feel they are losing control of life. Depression causes them to withdraw, to internalize and lose interest in activities they would ordinarily enjoy.

A person in this frame of mind will often refuse help or not respond as we would wish. But there are concrete things we can do to overcome the barriers and avoid pitfalls that could trip up our efforts. Barriers can be overcome when we recognize them and choose to respond effectively with love.

So let's look at a few barriers. And let's consider how our personal commitment can take shape in natural but sometimes daring ways— simple actions that are also potent gifts that can overcome barriers to freedom and healing.

Feeling Like an Object and Losing Control

Our sense of identity and value is either nurtured or undermined by our circumstances and how people treat us in them. With less and less control over what is happening to and around them, a sufferer often feels diminished, less like a person and more like an object.

For example, granted that modern medicine is a marvelous blessing, hospital treatment nevertheless can contribute to a sense of isolation. In a serious case, wires and tubes are everywhere. Vital though they are to sustain the patient, he or she can begin to feel like someone in a cage—on display but out of touch. Time drifts by in a peculiar, unmeasured pace far different from the patient's normal life.

Much depends on the bedside manner of practitioners. A patient is a person, not a project or an item of interest. A doctor or nurse who shows genuine care and interest in the patient's feelings humanizes the relationship, and in doing so often enhances the effectiveness of treatment. Expert care should not diminish one's value as a human being.

Richard

Richard was in the hospital again. He was in his late forties. When he was seventeen, Richard became ill with a condition that enflames the lining of his intestine, usually the large bowel first. Till then he had been a healthy and vigorous student and enjoyed playing football. But his condition turned into a chronic illness that led to several surgeries to treat, and later remove, portions of his digestive tract.

It did not end there. Richard developed ileitis, a disease in which parts of the small intestine occasionally become raw and bleeding, especially when a person is overly stressed. The result was that Richard was hospitalized at least a couple times a year to get his condition back under control.

Despite his limitation, Richard excelled in college. He once commented, "When I read something, it all seems to stick in my mind," probably indicating a photographic memory. Never studying for tests, he chose rather to read extra material. He consistently achieved a high grade point average.

Richard got married after college and proceeded toward a PhD in English at a large state university, where a teaching assistantship allowed him to teach creative writing to freshmen. He had a couple good years, but medical emergencies interrupted more and more frequently. Eventually the department head told Richard he should accept that his poor health prevented him from completing his doctorate. His supervisor affirmed that Richard had the intelligence and ability to be an excellent teacher, but his physical stamina was not sufficient. He could finish the year, and then he would be awarded a master's degree instead.

About the same time came the devastating revelation that Richard's wife was involved with another man. Wanting to be free of Richard and his problems, she divorced him and married her new love—the man Richard thought was his best friend. Richard felt doubly deceived, abandoned and betrayed.

Richard's losses were multilayered. First went his health. Then his postgraduate studies were cut short, and his dream of a prestigious doctoral degree and the opportunity to teach at a college came to an end.[7] So too, concurrently, did his marriage and the companionship of both his wife and his best friend. His achievement of a master's degree notwithstanding, he slipped into a state of chronic depression. Moving to a nearby city where an old college friend lived, Richard made a few contacts with high schools but had no success in getting a teaching job. It was the end of his teaching career. Out of desperation, he got a job as a custodian in a grade school. He could at least be among teachers. But this too soon turned sour after just a few months when his absences due to hospitalization caused his employer to let him go.

A few years later, during a hospitalization, Richard's chronic intestinal problem was complicated by a broken hip. Long-term steroid use for his ileitis had resulted in osteoporosis, weakening his bones. Two physicians attended him. One of them, an internist concerned with keeping his patient's digestive system in balance, Richard described like this: "When he comes in, he looks at my chart, does a little poking around, and leaves. Sometimes he hardly says a word or asks a question. I feel like he sees me as a machine and he is checking the oil level or something."

At such times Richard felt like he was no longer a real human being. Instead, he said, he felt like he was someone's long-term medical experiment. Losing his health, career, marriage, and friends had worn him out. He wrote in his journal, "Dear God, a long time ago I gave my life to you and now I want to run from it, escape it. I suffer pain every day. Worst of all, I'm getting nowhere."

Richard's experience reveals a barrier closely related to feeling like an object. It is the loss of control often felt by people with health troubles or other serious problems. Seasoned, well-trained nursing staff make extra efforts to explain things to patients and ask their permission whenever possible. But the feeling of losing control of one's life remains an invisible affliction on top of the medical condition.

♥

Learning that our health is seriously threatened is terrifying. It's like a sly enemy has undone our powers. We make every effort to regain some sense of control over our lives, but it's not always possible. Modern medicine sometimes even seems to demand that we give up control.

Imagine yourself in an intensive care unit. A nurse attendant comes in and says, "We're going to suction your lungs now so you can breathe better." No matter how caring that person's attitude is, he or she is not asking your permission—they are telling you what is going to happen. The treatment is necessary, and its goal is to preserve your health and restore your strength and freedom. But right now your autonomy is gone, and that can be frightening. Your personhood is diminished simply by cooperating with therapy.

Isolation and Loneliness

Sufferers often feel as though they are in a bubble of unreality, looking through a thick lens at the people who visit and at the world around them. It's difficult to focus on people's words. Emotions seem flat and meaningless. Being physically cut off from the normal world can be keenly painful.

Some sufferers have few visitors. For others, the visitors they have bring little solace because their comments are so superficial, while the patient's concerns are deep and disturbing. Loneliness persists because "nobody really understands." The distance between the sufferer and the normal world is such that he or she doesn't connect well even when visitors or caregivers try earnestly to communicate.

The more confusing the circumstances, the likelier the sufferer is to feel isolated and lonely. In a time of deep frustration or pain, he or she may think, "I don't know how to explain this. I feel so defeated. I don't know what to say, and nobody would understand anyway." Sufferers often feel embarrassed by their weakness when illness strikes. The condition may be only temporary, and healing will come with proper treatment and time. But at the time, it may seem like illness and pain define a person's life.

All this makes the work of the caregiver that much more challenging. Pay careful attention to the other person's every gesture and listen carefully to their words. Don't be put off by their lack of enthusiasm; persist in being fully present. Choosing to know and wanting to understand someone's life can be a profound gift. Suffering need not define the person; rather, it is a window through which you can become acquainted with him or her on a deeper level. And your effort to do so can help break that person free from their sense of isolation. Telling them, "It's okay to feel the way you do," validates them, and they can begin to better cope with their situation.

You may have options to suggest that the person might not have considered. But do so tentatively. Your first goal is to connect, not prescribe solutions or give advice that may not be welcome.

We surmount the barrier of isolation with gentleness. Specific suggestions for doing so will come up in the next chapter.

Joel

Joel was an active husband and father in his midforties. He loved hiking mountain trails with his teenage son and biking to work in good weather. As a computer technician, he enjoyed friendly relationships with his coworkers. His health had been stable and strong all his adult life. Then he was hit with a growing ache that just would not go away. A trip to the emergency room quickly led to a diagnosis of appendicitis and to surgery within twenty-four hours.

After discharge, Joel settled in at home for a quick recovery. But he was surprised at how tired and weak he was. Within a few days he was doing some of his computer tech work from home online or by phone, even though his energy level ran down in just a couple hours.

About the time when Joel expected to be back to full strength, pain slowly began to return, and he felt nauseous for hours. Another trip to the hospital revealed that a large abscess had developed. Joel would need a second surgery to clean it out. After several days in the hospital he was sent home with a drainage tube and collection bag.

During the rest of the week, Joel was so tired that he shut off his cell phone because he didn't have the energy for a conversation. And a couple weeks later, the familiar pain began to return. Soon Joel was in the hospital for the third time. He was assured that this kind of thing happens from time to time. His wife, knowing he would need some connections with their family home, hurried there with their son, gathered familiar pictures and flowers, and brought them back to Joel's hospital room. This time the treatment was a success. Joel returned to full health a few weeks later and regained his usual vigor.

Looking back at that time, Joel says, "I felt like I was on a different planet. Nothing was going right for me. I was away from my family and my work, and my health seemed to have deserted me. I felt like I had suddenly slipped from young adulthood into old age. Besides that, I didn't have the energy to talk to my friends who wanted to call. It was a really weird, alien experience."

He felt like he had made a trip to a foreign land and lost his passport. "You are stuck. Your identity is in question. You cannot go to work. And during hours of inactivity and depression, you slip easily into irrational and depressing thoughts. Missing work starts you thinking that perhaps you are not needed."

Joel had tried to go in to work on a few of his better days, but he felt like a "wimp" to come in late, maybe around 10:00 a.m., and then leave early at 2:30 in the afternoon. He continues, "I couldn't believe I had been sick for almost two months! I had been so frustrated and depressed, I didn't want to talk to people at times. I just wanted to curl up in a ball and sleep."

If recovering from a routine appendectomy can turn out to be so distressing, consider what the advent of terminal illness can do to someone.

Loneliness at the End of Life

In her landmark research with dying patients, Elizabeth Kübler-Ross showed that people who are dying often feel isolated and cut off from others, even when people are present. Kübler Ross and Carl Nighswonger interviewed several hundred patients, many of whom were terminally ill, plus family members and staff at University of Chicago Hospital during the late 1960s. They also paid careful attention to nurses and visitors calling on patients who were terminally ill. They noticed a couple of lamentable features.

First, they observed that the time it took for a nurse to respond to a patient call button grew longer after a patient was recognized as terminal. Second, most visitors spent less time with the patient. These two facts probably stemmed from the increasing discomfort that both professional staff and visitors felt dealing with a hopeless situation.

A third important item also came to light: Doctors frequently informed families and friends that a patient's illness was terminal, but they chose not to tell the patient. The doctors did not want the patient to give up hope, or they believed the patient was too weak to bear the bad news. Doctors are trained to heal, and an illness that could not be cured seemed like a failure. Their personal discomfort led them to avoid having a painful but honest conversation with the patient.

But when terminal patients were carefully interviewed, most said they had already discerned the truth. They noticed how the behavior of staff and visitors had changed toward them, and besides guessing the terminal nature of their condition, they experienced a deepening isolation. Their closest relationships were now stretched thin because a profound truth remained unspoken, considered off-limits. The denial of family members and doctors added to the dying person's pain and loneliness; trusted family and professionals were being false, disingenuous, thus distancing themselves from the patient. No one seemed willing to talk about the things that were most important to the patient, about that person's feelings and final wishes.[8]

Linda

Linda was a teacher in her midforties who had three sons, ages sixteen, twenty, and twenty-three, and a husband who loved her. Linda enjoyed nothing more than giving children the excitement of learning in creative ways. But she had to take leave of absence due to a pain that took much too long to diagnose properly. Finally it became clear that she had a form of cancer, and treatments ensued. She hoped to return to the school room, but slowly that hope grew dim.

Although the cancer was treated, it was never stopped. Linda gained some relief and hope with every round of therapy, but it was not long before something new began to appear. Back pains turned out to be a new cancer site that also required treatment. Linda was getting worn down. After the most recent setback, she spent a few weeks in a nursing center that provided vocational rehabilitation. But pain defeated most of the attempts to help Linda regain some independence. Pain medication now dulled her perceptions and hopes as well.

After a few particularly painful days, Linda was back at the hospital, and family members were informed that there was no longer hope for recovery. But her physician counseled them not to share this with Linda but rather to let things develop. She seemed content with the daily visits from her husband, her grown children, and her sister. Some days, though, the pain medications made her confused about even the most ordinary details.

One afternoon Linda's sister, Mary, was there by herself. After a few minutes of casual talk, Mary broached the difficult subject. "The doctors don't think you'll recover," she said. "Linda, you are dying."

Linda's response took Mary by surprise: "Thank God. I knew it but didn't think you did." It was a breakthrough moment of loving honesty. And now at last came the tears and the heart-rending sobs.

After that brief exchange, the conversations Mary and the rest of the family had with Linda were much more relaxed and enjoyable. They shared stories from childhood. They laughed together. With all the family around Linda's bed, they shared memories, spoke of regrets, sometimes asked for forgiveness, and most of all expressed love. They cried together too. Linda died a few days later.

Linda's sister said it was as if Linda was waiting for that time of confronting the truth and living in the moments left. They had broken through the silence and found the freedom to really enjoy each other once again. There were not many days left, but the ones that were, were precious and sweet.

Honest Treatment

Today's medical staff are better prepared to respond to patients' needs. In many medical centers, the family of a terminally ill patient will meet with a team consisting of a doctor, social worker, and clergy. The doctor may be a specialist in palliative care whose aim is to relieve pain and maximize the patient's comfort rather than try to treat a disease that cannot be cured. The medical social worker will often coach the family on how to discuss the matter with their dying loved one.

Unfortunately, this strategic support is not universal. Some medical doctors still conceal the truth from the terminally ill. Doctors are trained primarily to diagnose illness and then treat it. Dr. Atul Gawande describes how, in the face of terminal disease, doctors often maintain the attitude that they must treat whatever parts of the disease they still can, regardless of whether their effort will provide an extension of life with quality living. The disease becomes an opponent to fight to the end. For these doctors, giving up is admitting defeat.

In his book *Being Mortal*, Gawande calls for doctors and health-care providers to acknowledge that death is a natural part of life's sequence. So when further treatment is futile and may even diminish quality of life during the time a patient has left, a wise physician will recommend palliative care and appropriate choices for the family and patient to consider.[9]

Someone facing terminal illness is often told, "We need to move you to a different facility where you can be cared for." But if given some choice of where, when, and how this happens, the patient can maintain a better sense of control and personal value.

These challenges are daunting for families to manage. Families vary in culture, emotional intelligence, and maturity. Individuals are often unprepared for such emotionally draining responsibilities. Therefore, it is all the more important that the family's pastor or volunteer caregiver be sensitive to the painful challenge now involved.

As a caregiver or friend, we can be one of the sources of courage and confidence for the patient and the family.

A wise caregiver can help bridge the barriers between the dying person and reluctant family members who are grieving their loss. This is an opportunity to use gentle questions that open the door for honest conversation with the patient about his or her prognosis and the choices for treatment. For instance, "What do you think your chances of recovery are at this time?" "What does that mean to you?" "What questions do you have for the doctor or for us?"

The medical social worker or the caregiver can help the family by providing vocabulary for talking about palliative treatment and the services hospice care can provide. Learning to talk about the coming days or weeks can empower people to better consider home health-care alternatives or other facilities in a way that involves the patient and gives a level of comforting control to each person.

While we may have been focused on prolonging life for the person we love, his or her priorities may be very different. Dr. Gawande says, "People with serious illness have priorities besides simply prolonging their lives. Surveys find that their top concerns include avoiding suffering, strengthening relationship with family and friends, being mentally aware, not being a burden on others, and achieving a sense that their life is complete."[10] Besides this, many people who are firm in their faith are ready to welcome the end of life on this earth when it can no longer be fruitful but, rather, is becoming a series of painful or frustrating treatments that do little to hold off the momentum of decline. A hospice nurse or volunteer can provide valuable coaching to help reach across the barriers that might exist.

Perhaps most importantly, by pursuing honest and engaging conversation, family and their dying loved one will frequently experience many days, weeks, or even months during which their relationships are deepened with the sense of sharing in a profound journey together. Family and friends can share in care, express the love they have for one another, and demonstrate their affection in all sorts of caring ways. Strained relationships are frequently healed. This gives the dying one peace, love, and courage so the whole of life can be embraced in spite of the shortness of life.[11]

We have given considerable attention to the challenge of end-of-life communication because we will all face it in some way at some time. We can be part of honest and encouraging conversations that change seemingly hopeless situations into opportunities for grace, peace, and resolution. You and I can be better prepared if we learn the practices of honest and gracious engagement Jesus demonstrated. He has shown us some practical things we can learn to do in the presence of someone who is hurting. But first, let's consider one more common situation where alienation comes up.

Alienation during Marital Breakdown

Someone whose marriage is in trouble will often experience something similar to the terminal patient. People in this situation often feel like matters are going beyond their control. Conflicting parties, attorneys, and the court itself seem to be in charge. The person's attorney may be calling the shots for them, making decisions they don't fully understand. The person may feel like they are on a dim pathway through an alien land of legal maneuvering. Less scrupulous attorneys seem to treat divorcing clients with a routine approach that prioritizes the lawyer's professional goals rather than those of the client.

The separated or divorced individual will often notice changes in how people treat them. Some acquaintances are themselves in pain because two people they care about are having a marriage breakdown. The husband and wife in a dissolving marriage often find that people who have been part of their life subtly change their habits. A friend seems extra busy and doesn't have time for lunch this week. Couples who often socialize with the divorcing persons don't know which to invite, so they speak to neither. Unsure what to say, they simply stay away. But by saying and doing nothing, they compound the pain of those in marital trouble. In chapter 2, I shared how one couple provided profound relief and encouragement for my wife and me when our own marriage was heading toward divorce. But such engagement is all too rare.

Often nothing at all is said about the elephant in the room. The separated persons may need to talk about their situation, but no one mentions it. One woman who was experiencing her marriage breaking up had the courage to ask a member of her church about this silence. "We didn't want to make you feel bad," the person said.

"But I already feel bad," she replied. "It would have helped to talk about it with somebody!"

Conversation may be difficult, but it is all the more valuable because it is full of heartfelt concerns. We don't need to have solutions to difficult questions; we just need a heart for listening. We can accept the feelings expressed without offering pat answers. Paying attention without judging is a powerful way to give value and respect that build up a person for the long, slow marathon of healing that lies ahead.

Sometimes conversation comes to a halt. Then, a friend who has no agenda except to be present is a precious gift. We can bring comfort even in the silence just by being there. The separated or divorced person may feel distant from everyone, but a simple touch, holding the person's hand, can be all it takes to bridge the barrier. When isolation and loneliness threaten, the greatest gift you can give is simply yourself and your time.

The challenge may seem daunting, but the rewards are precious. You can participate in another person's intimate journey toward acceptance, resolution, and wholeness. And those involved will express their gratitude for your part in helping them.

Gifts that Break the Barriers

The world is full of people with their own agenda, even when dealing with the suffering. The minister who arrives with a canned message designed to manipulate the sufferer to some particular expression of faith is only following his own most comfortable path. We as caregivers must be alert to our tendencies and scrutinize our personal goals and motives.

Jesus showed a remarkable ability to engage individuals without a hidden agenda. His actions were honest and expressed his care with integrity. Of course, he performed miracles with an authority that none of us can imitate. But other things that he did are totally within our own scope, and we can follow his pattern.

How did Jesus come into contact with the real-life challenges of his fellow human beings? How did he live out his incarnational lifestyle with people? What does his way of being in touch teach us about being a caring person?

Let's look at, and learn from, five powerful gifts Jesus exhibited for breaking through people's barriers of isolation and loneliness in order to bring healing in place of brokenness and restore dignity in place of diminishment.

The Gift of Tender Touch

> There was a man covered with leprosy. When he saw Jesus, he bowed with his face to the ground and begged him, "Lord, if you choose, you can make me clean." Then Jesus stretched out his hand, touched him, and said, "I do choose. Be made clean." Immediately the leprosy left him. (Luke 5:12–13 NRSV)

The man with leprosy hoped Jesus would heal him, but he never expected Jesus to touch him. Healthy people always stayed at a distance from lepers, afraid of catching the disease. Leprosy victims were accustomed to being cut off from normal human interaction, and Jesus knew this. He clearly chose to touch the man. The astonished onlookers must have been aghast. The man himself must have been astonished. Jesus's touch was a profound expression of the man's value in Jesus's eyes. Jesus recognized him as a human being, not a pariah to be feared. He was healed in body and no doubt given a wonderful healing of soul and identity as well.

Touching is a simple thing, yet fraught with potential for good or evil. When a person is hurting, how much a touch can communicate! In hospitals, the patients' favorite part of the day is often the time when they get a back rub. There are also those who aren't suffering physically but still are missing human touch. The loss of a mate after many years of companionship means the end of physical affection for the surviving spouse. Family or friends may attempt to fill the gap, but widowed persons nevertheless often express a keen sense of missing their spouse's touch. A widow once said to me, "Sunday at church is the only time I get a hug all week." I was glad to hear she at least got a hug there. Her connection to a caring community was affirmed weekly by this physical contact; it became another sacrament confirming her faith.

Some caution is necessary where physical touch is involved. Charges of sexual abuse are common, and it's good this offense is getting the public attention it deserves. But the downside is, a touch can be perceived in a way we do not intend. And there's another consideration: an ill person may be particularly touch-sensitive, to the point where a touch is painful.

Those concerns aside, touch is nevertheless a powerful means of communicating love to someone who is lonely, hurting, or gravely ill. The best approach is to ask permission: "Is it okay for me to hold your hand?" This shows both reasonable caution and respect for that individual's personal space.

Amanda

One of the most remarkable places I have ever visited is Joseph's House, a hospice facility specializing in serving homeless people with HIV/AIDS whose lives are nearing the end.[12] (In the United States, the CDC reports about 50% of all HIV/AIDS sufferers either were not in treatment during 2018 or were not continuing an effective treatment regimen due to homelessness, mental illness, or other complicating fathers.) I had been told that this outstanding facility engaged in a cutting edge ministry of mercy.

On a shady street in Washington, DC, I arrived at the address and found a beautiful three-story brick home that must have been built in the Victorian era. No doubt it once had been a spacious residence for someone of means.

Having made an appointment to interview some of the staff, I was cordially welcomed after I knocked at the heavy oak door. During my brief welcome conversation, I learned they were caring for eight men at the time, and their capacity was limited to ten. Most of the time the home was full.

Amanda, one of the nurse assistants, exuded a joy that flooded out easily. She was about forty and had worked there for nearly ten years. She described her responsibilities there and told me how much the residents appreciated good care. They were mostly people who had nothing and no one, and frequently they had only days or weeks to live. What she told me next amazed me.

When their patients arrived, Amanda said, they were nearing the limits of their resistance to intestinal infections or pneumonia. Diarrhea and vomiting were common, and it was routine for staff to wear rubber gloves for all manner of contact with residents. Yet, with a touch of delight, Amanda continued:

> Yes, we're supposed to wear gloves all the time. And I do most of the time. But now and then, when I can see that one of our residents has no lesions and doesn't seem to harbor much risk for me, I'll take the gloves off and give him a really good back rub. You know, there's just no substitute for skin on skin. I know it's risky, but I just love these people too much to not do it. I know how much they need it.

Her compassion soared beyond medical protocol with remarkably unselfish, godly, and risky love. This wonderful person was living out Jesus's pattern of touching someone whom others would avoid. She felt compelled to offer love and compassion with touch while fully aware of the risks. She chose to take the risk for the sake of love. While she told me about this, I knew I was looking into the eyes of a Jesus follower.

On many other occasions, with little or no risk, we can touch someone in a meaningful way. During prayer with someone who is ill, whenever possible, touching a hand or shoulder is an important way to connect and communicate our solidarity with that person as we come before God. We also communicate the touch of God as we represent the grace of God and his care for that person. If there is the slightest doubt about whether it will be welcome, we should always ask, "Is it all right with you if I hold your hand (or touch your shoulder) while we pray?"

The Gift of Conversation That Connects

Jesus, resting by a well in Samaria while his disciples went off to buy food, initiates a conversation with an unlikely person.

> When a Samaritan woman came to draw water, Jesus said to her, "Will you give me a drink?" . . .
>
> The Samaritan woman said to him, "You are a Jew and I am a Samaritan woman. How can you ask me for a drink?" (For Jews do not associate with Samaritans.)
>
> Jesus answered her, "If you knew the gift of God and who it is that asks you for a drink, you would have asked him and he would have given you living water."
>
> "Sir," the woman said, "you have nothing to draw with and the well is deep. Where can you get this living water? Are you greater than our father Jacob, who gave us the well and drank from it himself, as did also his sons and his flocks and his livestock?"

Jesus answered, "Everyone who drinks this water will be thirsty again, but whoever drinks the water I give them will never thirst. Indeed, the water I give them will become in them a spring of water welling up to eternal life."

The woman said to him, "Sir, give me this water so that I won't get thirsty and have to keep coming here to draw water."

He told her, "Go, call your husband and come back."

"I have no husband," she replied.

Jesus said to her, "You are right when you say you have no husband. The fact is, you have had five husbands, and the man you now have is not your husband. What you have just said is quite true."

"Sir," the woman said, "I can see that you are a prophet." (John 4:7, 9–19)

At this point the woman turns the subject away from herself and brings up their differences in where and how to worship, whether in Jerusalem or at the temple in Samaria. But Jesus brings the conversation to a disclosure of startling directness and intimacy.

[Jesus said,] "God is spirit, and his worshipers must worship in the spirit and in truth."

The woman said, "I know that Messiah (called Christ) is coming. When he comes, he will explain everything to us."

Then Jesus declared, "I, the one speaking to you—I am he."

Just then his disciples returned and were surprised to find him talking with a woman. But no one asked, "What do you want?" or "Why are you talking with her?"

Then, leaving her water jar, the woman went back to the town and said to the people, "Come, see a man who told me everything I ever did. Could this be the Messiah?" (John 4:24–29)

The woman's neighbors avoid her because of her bad reputation. Jesus, on the other hand, surprises her by asking for a drink of water. He knows about rejection firsthand from his own experience at the synagogue in his hometown of Nazareth (Mark 6:2–3). He is well acquainted with the painful feeling of alienation. He doesn't mind being seen talking with the woman, and his conversation with her communicates acceptance and selfless love. Jesus talks with her about what really matters in her life. He willingly listens to her spiritual concerns, but he also redirects the conversation to her most pressing personal problem: her life of rejection by several husbands and the ostracism by her neighbors. Then at the culmination of their dialogue, with unprecedented directness, he reveals his true identity to her.

Notice how Jesus starts casually and then pursues deeper matters.

1. Jesus speaks to a stranger who does not expect any conversation.

2. First he asks for help, expressing his need for a drink.

3. In response to the woman's surprise due to their different cultures, Jesus intrigues her with a clue about his identity.

4. The woman expresses her own need, albeit obliquely: "Sir, give me this water so that I won't get thirsty."

5. Responding to her yearning, Jesus risks addressing an uncomfortable part of her life—her many husbands and current partner.

6. The woman turns the subject to theoretical—and safer—questions about their religious differences, but Jesus won't be deterred. To her attempt to hide, he responds with a startling self-disclosure.

7. The result is a revolution in the woman's life, as described in the latter part of chapter four in John's gospel.

Unfortunately, we often avoid such a dynamic encounter when we meet someone in need. People sometimes make well-intentioned visits to a sufferer, but are stymied about what to say or do. Of course, just the presence of a caring person is often very much welcome and appreciated. And talking about the ordinary things of life can be enjoyable. But sometimes discussion of baseball or the weather becomes a thin substitute for actual encounter. And eventually the hurting person hears, "Well, I've got to go." Sometimes the sufferer and the visitor are both eager to be relieved of the vague tension of being near but not really in touch, not talking about things that matter most.

Naturally we may be uncomfortable with the facts. We cannot make someone's pain go away. But our own discomfort mirrors that of the other person, whose situation we cannot immediately improve. When it is medically hopeless, the pressure is worse. Even a short-term illness can be painful and cause the sick person considerable distress. As a result we may feel ill at ease and wish we could get away. We must be prepared to listen to things we do not want to hear. The hurting person's issues must be our focus, not our own agenda. We may fear facing questions we cannot answer and feeling inadequate. We may worry that our attempts to encourage will be rejected. We have to overcome these feelings and risk the real involvement necessary to reach across the patient's barriers.*

Richard's Other Doctor

Richard, the long-suffering patient we described a few pages back, had a second doctor, an orthopedic surgeon, who performed the surgical repair for Richard's hip. He seemed to recognize the complicated nature of Richard's medical problems and that Richard might never again be well enough to walk unaided. This doctor took time to gently explain the prognosis to Richard. Richard described the surgeon this way: "He stops in at the end of his long day to ask how my physical therapy is going. But we also talk about poetry and politics, about his hobbies and his family. I think he enjoys seeing me, for some reason."

Having someone like this doctor take time to show interest in his life and the things Richard especially appreciated, poetry and

---

*Resources and exercises to improve your listening and conversation skills and build your confidence can be found in appendix A.

writing, was a special gift. Many busy physicians and nurses cannot take a lot of time to visit like this surgeon did. His visits contrasted starkly with the cold, clinical approach of Richard's internist.

That contrast illuminates a disadvantage inherent in modern medicine. Specialists are under pressure to deal with many patients in a limited time. They can be tempted to look at only a part of the picture, although they certainly know that everything about a patient is related. In the same way, we as visitors are tempted to limit our time and may slip into a "formula" that is less than a full engagement with the hurting person. How we interact is critical. Showing genuine appreciation for that person and his or her unique life can have a potent effect.

Any visitor who took the time to ask Richard about his life, his education, and his interests would have learned a great deal. Richard had taught creative writing. He had a photographic memory and could converse intelligently on almost any subject. Fortunately, he had a few friends who shared his interest in literature and writing. Their visits were a lifeline to Richard while he was "at sea" in the slow process of healing.

------- ♥ -------

Severe medical problems can quickly lead to situational depression. In response, the sufferer may withdraw from those who might help them. Depressed persons often conclude they aren't worth other people's attention. Who would want to talk with them about their troubles? To the patient, it's all embarrassing and frustrating. In this downward spiral, the barriers, real and imaginary, spring up to isolate them.

The psalm writer captures that feeling: "You have taken my companions and loved ones from me; the darkness is my closest friend" (Psalm 88:18 NIV 1984). Other personal setbacks can generate the same effect.

Jesus was known on more than one occasion to ask a person, "What do you want me to do for you?" He did not assume that the visible circumstance revealed the problem most dear to that person's heart. He talked. He asked questions. He engaged in conversation that brought hope and healing.

The Gift of Daring Presence

The deeper and more confusing the occasion, whether it's an illness or a social or moral failure, the likelier it is that isolation or loneliness will envelope a person. Jesus dared to throw over this barrier.

> While Jesus was having dinner at Levi's house, many tax collectors and sinners were eating with him and his disciples, for there were many who followed him. When the teachers of the law who were Pharisees saw him eating with the sinners and tax collectors, they asked his disciples: "Why does he eat with tax collectors and sinners?" (Mark 2:15–16)

Jesus was willing to sit down with those whom most of society despised because of their status, their power, and their association with a foreign occupying force.

On another occasion, while Jesus was having dinner with a more respectable set, some religious Pharisees, he broke a societal norm by accepting the gratitude of a despised, outcast woman.

> When one of the Pharisees invited Jesus to have dinner with him, he went to the Pharisee's house and reclined at the table. A woman in that town who lived a sinful life learned that Jesus was eating at the Pharisee's house, so she came there with an alabaster jar of perfume. As she stood behind him at his feet weeping, she began to wet his feet with her tears. Then she wiped them with her hair, kissed them and poured perfume on them.
>
> When the Pharisee who had invited him saw this, he said to himself, "If this man were a prophet, he would know who is touching him and what kind of woman she is—that she is a sinner." (Luke 7:36–39)

Jesus was eager to meet people whose lives were distorted by trouble, by failure, by sin, and by social ostracism. Just as he surprised the Samaritan woman who met him at Jacob's well, Jesus frequently broke through the barriers people experience. Ostracism may be practiced with more subtlety in our day, but the results are the same. Someone in trouble is avoided by others. People stay away, and the person, who already feels like a failure, is further burdened with rejection and alienation.

Yet on the other hand, sometimes a few brave people recognize the opportunity to bring hope and healing.

Five Brave Men

In a small Michigan town, a few men gathered weekly for breakfast and prayer. They were mostly community leaders, including business owners, educators, and professionals plus one man from their church who was less educated, often struggled financially, and was not known for good judgment. But he yearned to be a faithful and successful person, and his companions knew he was sincere. They met for fellowship and prayer over several years and saw each other at church as well.

Then a grim failure came to light. The man confessed to them a criminal sexual offense he had recently committed. He knew he would soon be arrested and most likely receive a prison sentence. He came to them to express his repentance and ask for their prayers. Although his offense was of a lesser degree legally, many in the village and at his church were appalled. But it was his first offence, and his prayer partners refused to ostracize him. Some of them appeared at his arraignment, at which he pled guilty. After arraignment he was free on bond for a short time, and each of his fellow prayer partners did what he could to encourage and support him. Two more appeared in court to encourage him when he was sentenced.

One of the men paid for a newspaper subscription for the offender, so he received a daily edition while in state prison for two years. Group members paid him occasional visits even though the prison was a couple hours away. When he was released and in need of a job, one of the businessmen offered him a job at a nearby town where he could work without daily encountering people who still despised him.

What is remarkable is how this man's five friends risked their public standing. Each man had a position of leadership and respect in the community, and certainly they all wished to maintain that respect. But they chose to risk offering grace and mercy to someone whom others despised. They believed their brother had come clean to them and repented of his sin. They took the chance of associating with him and risking the disfavor of many others in the town.

But while some in the village surely doubted these men's choice, their stature in the community didn't suffer. In fact, some people respected them even more. They had shown the offender grace yet at the same time held him accountable. After his term in prison he returned to a life of responsibility and faithfulness, in part because of his friends' willingness to associate with the lowly. They dared to be present with him when he needed friends the most.

The Gift of Vulnerability

Jesus's friends Martha and Mary were in despair when Jesus made no effort to get to Bethany before his friend Lazarus died. The account in John 11:6 says, "When he heard that Lazarus was sick, he stayed where he was two more days." Jesus seems to have purposely delayed his coming until Lazarus had died.

Martha and Mary each in turn confronted him with their disappointment.

> When Mary reached the place where Jesus was and saw him, she fell at his feet and said, "Lord, if you had been here, my brother would not have died."
>
> When Jesus saw her weeping, and the Jews who had come along with her also weeping, he was deeply moved in spirit and troubled. "Where have you laid him?" he asked.

"Come and see, Lord," they replied.

Jesus wept.

Then the Jews said, "See how he loved him!"

But some of them said, "Could not he who opened the eyes of the blind man have kept this man from dying?" (John 11:32–37)

We might have scolded him too. But when they arrived at the tomb, something happened that spoke to their complaint. The English translation of the verse that describes it, verse 33, is weak; the original language suggests something deeper, such as "he began to shake and snort, being disturbed so deeply, shaken in his spirit." And the verse "Jesus wept" speaks volumes to us, as it did to the bystanders: "See how he loved him!"

Jesus was not cool and aloof in spite of the powers he had. He was not immune to the emotions that tear at us when we know a friend has suffered. Jesus wept for his friend Lazarus and his sisters. Jesus was so deeply imbedded in humanity that he lived and experienced grief, even though he could call on the powers of heaven to restore Lazarus. Tears communicated his love.

Once again Jesus sets an example worth studying. Why is it that we who would minister to others fight to avoid the tears? No doubt we want to avoid the appearance of losing control. We want to perform our duties, be coherent, be respected. But if we appear unmoved in the presence of someone's deep grief or pain, our "professionalism" might seem to lack compassion. It's all right to cry. It communicates your sensitivity and is one more form of honesty. It communicates love.

There will be times and places when we need to rein in our emotions to avoid distracting others and complicating the situation. But consider: When we ourselves bear great pain and sorrow, and we see emotion in the eyes of a friend, a caregiver, even a doctor or nurse, we will likely appreciate their compassion. When eyes turn glassy and tears are near, we interpret that to mean the person feels moved. If we can likewise learn to show our own emotions without fear, our words of sympathy or comfort are all the likelier to be appreciated. The more we get beyond ourselves, the more we can trust God to be the one in control. Sometimes tears speak greater messages of God's love than words.

The Powerless Pastor

When I was a young and inexperienced pastor, I once was given a sudden and terrible responsibility. A young man from our church was serving in the military, and he was involved in combat in a war zone. One morning I got a call from a man who identified himself as an Army officer. He asked whether I was the pastor of the serviceman's family. Then he told me the soldier had been severely wounded, and he gave me the awful details. He asked me to immediately head to the parents' home to await the arrival of Army personnel to tell them the news. I hung up the phone, I wept, and I prayed.

I set out on my errand of mercy with deep dread. These parents were among the kindest, most loving people I had come to know at my church. As I drove, waves of emotion swept over me, bringing one flood of tears after another. The news was dreadful: shrapnel wounds throughout the extremities, severe head wounds, probable loss of eyesight, possible brain damage. My chest felt like a lead weight was bearing down on my heart.

When I arrived, the mother was outside working in the yard. She greeted me with her usual jovial warmth. Then her face took on an anxiously questioning look. I could hardly open my mouth. "It's about your son" I said. She was frozen by my words and erupted in tears.

Her husband was working not far away. We called him home, and I related what I had been told. The gruesome words fell like rocks. For long moments we sat, often without words, sometimes in prayer, many times in tears. I had few words to offer and could not help but cry with them. The officers soon arrived and confirmed my words. More long moments passed as we prayed to seek God's comfort in the midst of tears.

We were told that a more conclusive medical evaluation would come in a few days. After some anxious waiting, the reports began to get better little by little. In a few weeks, their son was flown to the States. He remained in military hospitals for nearly two years and endured multiple surgeries. His parents traveled the several hundred miles to see him as often as they could.

After rehabilitation, the young man did come home. His vision was intact, his mind healthy, and his body whole enough for a normal life, regardless of some small evidences of reconstructive surgery. But I've never forgotten that awful day. My relationship with that special family henceforth had a heartfelt tenderness forged by the tears we shared. The experience changed me. Being near them in such intense pain revealed to me a form of ministry that went beyond knowing the right words and prayers. It had more to do with actually being *with* people in weakness and suffering.

I learned that when we endure deep pain and sorrow with someone, we become bonded at a profound level that is never forgotten. We became more open to feeling others' pain and offering more compassionate responses. Finally, I realized that shedding tears does not make us look weak in others' eyes; rather, it makes our compassion evident, and whatever words we say become more trustworthy because we have suffered together.

Our willingness to be with someone in trouble and feel their pain communicates our genuine concern and love. And this in turn generates courage. A supervisor of social workers at a large Veterans Administration hospital told me, "I try to teach our people that we have to be willing to climb into that barrel of pain with [our patients]. We do need to maintain objectivity, of course. But unless we crawl into their barrel of pain, you're not going to do them much good." Someone else might call it walking together on holy ground.

The Gift of Going to the Edge

Cheryl is a social worker with patients who often have debilitating neurological diseases. She meets with them, and their families as well, during visits. She says their fear of what is to come sometimes can just about paralyze them. They find it hard to make decisions and hard to reconcile their broken dreams. She tells them, "I'm somebody to walk with you when nobody wants to walk with you." The more dismal and ugly the circumstances, the less likely we want to be around them. But Jesus followed through to the finish.

> Two other men, both criminals, were also led out with him to be executed. When they came to the place called the Skull, they crucified him there, along with the criminals—one on his right, the other on his left. Jesus said, "Father, forgive them, for they do not know what they are doing." . . .
>
> One of the criminals who hung there hurled insults at him: "Aren't you the Messiah? Save yourself and us!"
>
> But the other criminal rebuked him. "Don't you fear God," he said, "since you are under the same sentence? We are punished justly, for we are getting what our deeds deserve. But this man has done nothing wrong."
>
> Then he said, "Jesus, remember me when you come into your kingdom."
>
> Jesus answered him, "Truly I tell you, today you will be with me in paradise." (Luke 23:32–34, 39–43)

One dying man asks a favor of another dying man. Jesus was in his own hour of agony and humiliation. But by being there, he was available for the criminal to know him. He was now part of that special group of people the Romans crucified. He was among criminals, spit upon, despised and rejected, as Isaiah's prophecy describes (Isaiah 53:3–9).

Though near to death Jesus still reaches out to encourage a man who is desperate and has no defenses left. The man's deepest desire is expressed by his request, "Lord, remember me." He has lost possessions, respect, and his friends, and now he is about to lose life itself, so caution goes to the wind. Jesus appreciates his honest desperation. In a way, Jesus's response says, "I have been with you in your reality, and now you will be with me in mine." He is with the criminal, the thief, the sinner in our fallen world, as with all of us, to the very end.

What does this tell us about caregiving? When the pain of moral failure, just like illness, seems to define our life, a friend who sticks with us gives a powerful gift. Few will stay with us when we are caught in a circumstance that seems like a dead end. But Jesus was with the criminal in the criminal's place. And he did not hesitate to identify the criminal as a new friend with whom he would spend his future.

Jesus lived his life to the fullest and to the depths. He was fully engaged, not watching out for comfort nor afraid of being misunderstood. He often *was* misunderstood. Jesus noted, "The Son of Man came eating and drinking, and they say, 'Here is a glutton and a drunkard, a friend of tax collectors and sinners'" (Matthew 11:19). But he was secure enough in himself that he could associate with all kinds of people. By being present, he shared his inner confidence and gave hope to those who were the target of other people's cruelty and spite. We prove ourselves to be genuine caregivers when we offer a sufferer the gift of going with them all the way to the edge.

Even Ordinary Gifts Have Power

Sensitive touch, conversation that connects, daring presence, honest tears, and staying to the finish—these five gifts are both powerful and simple. But they are not easy to give, nor are they easy for some people to receive. Sometimes more common gifts, the ordinary things we do, can move a relationship in the positive direction. A gift of flowers might brighten up the room for someone temporarily confined. Other practical gifts can show we care.

People often hesitate to ask for help with the ordinary things of life. When someone is worn out from trouble and pain, every worry seems overwhelming. By addressing practical matters, we can help relieve a person's mind. And most people who care and want to help will feel comfortable doing something concrete. There are many kinds of gifts people can give. How to get started?

We can ask practical questions. "Is there anything I can do?" is usually not going to create opportunities. But more specific questions can—questions like

- Is your house being taken care of?
- Do you need someone to cut grass, or rake leaves?
- Is your mail being collected?
- Do you need any clothes from home?
- Can I get you some special food you miss?

To discover a person's needs, we need to see the world as they do. What we would worry about if we were in his or her spot? We must pray to feel and see the world as that person does. Then our prayerful inquiries will lead to loving action.

A caring person can bring energy and encouragement by meeting needs and thus relieving the other person's worries. Such compassion fills a void. It demonstrates practical love. When we ask, we need to listen carefully for the answers, especially when someone hesitates to ask for help. Be persistent. Take the risk of asking. Perhaps we can't personally meet those needs, but we can call on others in our network of caring people who can help. We can respond, "I will find someone to take care of that for you."

Offering such practical gifts nurtures our connection and fosters trust. This in turn can open doors to help in other ways. It may lead to opportunities to offer the gifts of deeper conversation and presence at those ragged edges of life. Then the giving of ourselves becomes the medium for God's grace to transform times of pain into occasions for healing and hope.

Jesus Dared to Connect

To each person in this chapter's biblical encounters—to the marginalized man with leprosy; the lonely woman at the well; the grieving sisters, Martha and Mary; the tax collectors and sinners; and the dying thief on the cross—Jesus communicates, "I am willing to be with *you*. I am willing to touch you, be seen with you, talk with you, suffer with you. I am willing to feel what you are feeling." People who dare to be in touch with others' discomfort experience the pain but also the mysterious satisfaction that compassion produces.

Jesus communicated his solidarity with people in their particular kinds of suffering. He chose actions and an attitude of confident incarnation that expressed his unselfish love. His "being with" was revolutionary and life changing for those he encountered. And his life is a clear window for our view into God's tender, self-giving heart.

Jesus's compassion flowed out to the hurting and drew them into fellowship with him. The word *compassion* (Latin: *com passus*) means literally "to feel with," to be deeply moved by what another person is feeling. We are called to open ourselves to feel what the sufferer is feeling, to enter into that person's experience and express our solidarity with them in Christ.

Conclusion

The story is told of a reporter watching Mother Teresa wash a destitute patient covered with sores. The reporter commented, "I wouldn't do that for a million dollars." She is said to have replied, "I wouldn't either. But I can do it for love." The simple gifts that flow from compassion, like touch, conversation, and deeply entering another person's world, sometimes with tears, are potent ways of making God's love real for someone. You and I have opportunity to literally embody the presence of God and give the most precious gift of love itself.

In the next chapter we will look at how caregiving with such compassion leads to surprising blessings that flow both ways. Although you and I may be the active caregiver, the sufferer has much to offer us. There is much we can learn from them. We will explore how, when we enter another person's life through compassion, the simple gifts we offer can lead to profound blessings coming back to us.

FOR DISCUSSION OR PERSONAL REFLECTION

1 When you had an experience that stopped your life from going on the way you expected, how did your experiences of isolation, loneliness, or the feeling of losing control affect you?

2 Of the main caregiver "gifts" mentioned, which of them comes easily to you, and which would you find difficult to carry out?

3 In order for you to be effective reaching out to a suffering person, do you need training in skills like active listening, or deepening your walk with Jesus?

CHAPTER 4

The Blessings
Go Both Ways

KEY POINTS IN THIS CHAPTER

1 Ministry goes both ways, as sufferers often have valuable gifts to give the caregiver:

>Life lessons
>
>Friendship
>
>Healing
>
>More

2 The experience of mutual giving builds self-esteem and gives the sufferer a sense of purpose and usefulness.

3 Mutual giving and receiving is a godly way of living that mirrors the life of God and enriches our lives.

So far we have paid a lot of attention to the negative aspects of caregiving and how to surmount them. We have talked about boundaries and barriers and other challenges that can erode our courage when we need it most. But there is another side of the coin. Surprising blessings await us as well.

It's natural to think of ourselves as the ones who are giving. The process of caregiving may seem one-sided, a flow of energy, time, and attention going out from us toward someone in need. We may be tempted to expect nothing in return from the person being helped.

But that would be a mistake.

When we recognize that the one receiving our care has something to offer us as well, two things happen. First, we do that person a lot more good than if we expected nothing reciprocal from them. Second, we discover that the gifts flowing back to us enrich our lives as much or more than what we are giving.

In this chapter, we'll consider how this marvelous economy of blessings works.

Receiving Gifts from the Sufferer

Giving and receiving is the dynamic that distinguishes the best of human interactions. When we are healthy, it can be hard to receive from others, especially those whose vitality is diminished. But inside every wrinkled or disabled body is someone who has memories, curiosity, and a desire to express what is real or important to them. Even when some mental functions have declined, every person still wants to be known as a person, with the ability to give something to us. Simply by attending to someone with an attitude of openness, we can provide them with opportunities to share something with us. In this way we enter a relationship of mutual blessing that nurtures in both directions.

God's self-giving in the dynamic story of salvation is designed to draw us into a pattern of both giving ourselves to others and receiving from them. It's in this manner that we are drawn into a higher level of life and godliness. Salvation revolutionizes how we relate to people in all phases of life, and that includes suffering.

In her book *Why Is This Happening to Me?*, Erika Schuchardt shares the following unforgettable account of a pastoral candidate in Germany training for ministry. He was assigned to New Ebenezer, Ward 7, which served as a home for the incapacitated. Upon arrival on his first day, he was brought by the orderly, whose name was Hollan, to a patient's bed and told, "You can begin giving our Fritz a bath right away!"

"What I saw just about sent me out the door," the pastor recalled. "A completely deranged young man of 20, a bedsore-ridden bundle of skin and bones, whose knees were permanently drawn up to his armpits in a cramp."

The young pastor steeled his nerves and proceeded with the task, difficult as it was. When he finished about a quarter hour later, "this horrible bundle began to move and raised its arm. Frightened, I looked for Hollan, the orderly."

Hollan, who had been observing the process, came over and said, "Sir, can't you tell? Fritz wants to thank you!"

The pastor reflects, "I hadn't seen Fritz as a human being at all. How this sick man must have suffered as he noticed that I hadn't seen him as a human being, but as a disgusting object. Yet . . . he tried to find a way to help me . . . by thanking me. He, the sick and deranged man, was capable of being part of a community. I, the healthy person, was not, and it took his help for me to develop this capacity. We quickly became good friends."[13]

Charles Garfield, a pioneer in peer counseling and emotional support, reminds us that one of the greatest gifts we can give someone is time and opportunity for them to give to us.[14] What they offer may be small, perhaps a handmade craft item, or an even more personal gift such as their reading a favorite poem to us. Or they may share profound lessons learned from the troubles or victories they have experienced. We will miss out on a great deal if we fail to listen to the wisdom garnered by those who suffer.

Life Lessons

When we allow a sufferer to teach us something, we are complimenting them. We are saying, "There are things I don't know that perhaps you do know. Please share your knowledge with me." We are expressing appreciation of a person, not dealing with an object of need.

Mutuality is not something we are always comfortable with. But it can be a pathway for profound learning. One of my friends, a seminary professor, commenting on his affliction with a neurological disease and its likely progression, shared with me what he had told his students:

> A time will come when I will need you in different ways than I do now. A time may come when I cannot speak, and you will need to speak for me and listen to me in new ways. A time may come when I can no longer pray and you will need to do my praying for me. A time may come when I can no longer think, when I can no longer believe. You will need to do the believing for me. This is why we belong to each other in Christ. This is what the communion of the saints means. This is what the body of Christ means.

This man offered his students an unforgettable lesson. When we realize we are profoundly connected to the suffering of others, we glimpse our oneness in Christ. Just as we find out who God is in the context of deep relationships, so we also find out who we ourselves are. We understand the meaning of community, ourselves, and God together. Some followers of Christ have turned such experiences into an avenue of intimacy with God and service to God as well as a great source of joy and peace.

We can expect to receive blessings from people we are helping because they are unique creations of God. Their life experiences are not duplicated by anyone else. So we can encourage them to be a blessing to others. The church can better serve its senior citizens, its disabled persons, and those who are ill by expecting something of them. There is a wealth of wisdom, energy, and love which needs to be encouraged. The wonderful result is not just that we "get more done" but, rather, that the spiritual health of the whole body of Christ is enhanced. The sufferer engages in ministry and reaps the blessing of satisfaction. That is what happened with Helen.

Helen

I heard about Helen shortly after I moved in as pastor of a small country church. Her husband, Gene, was a regular at worship, but she was unable to attend. I learned that she was stricken with multiple sclerosis in her late forties. Over the next few years she became immobile and spent most of every day in bed. Her husband told me that, except for special occasions, Helen never left their home. Gene worked alone on their modest farm. While tending to his work, he said he could get back to the house often enough each day to see to her needs.

One afternoon I found the time to call Helen and schedule a visit. As I dialed the number, I thought how miserable I would feel in her situation. But I was surprised by the cheerful voice that greeted me. Helen told me she would warmly welcome a visit, and when I arrived I should just walk in since Gene would be working in the field.

So it was that I discovered a delightful and cheerful lady who, I learned as we talked, made phone calls every day to others in the church and community who were sick or disabled. She wrote cards and notes to hundreds of people every year, encouraging them if they were ill or simply wishing them a happy birthday or anniversary. Helen had a gift of encouragement, and she exercised it.

By the time I left, I did not feel at all worn down from giving her pastoral support; rather, I felt encouraged in the midst of my own challenges. Helen was that kind of lady. She continued for years in her remarkable ministry, a well-known blessing to people for miles around. She was a happy person. And she enriched my life whenever I saw her.

People who are suffering may have a story to tell. Often someone nearing the end of their life wants to share some precious memory. That story may have special meaning to them, and it can offer a gem of wisdom to you, the listener. The giver may not be thinking of it that way, but it is a precious gift. People who normally do not talk about their lives or reveal their inner thoughts sometimes do so as death draws closer. If you have shown interest and demonstrated God's love and care, you may be entrusted with thoughts they have shared with no one else. Don't be too busy to listen. Allow time for them to tell their story. It may be the most interesting part of your day.

Friendship

When we give of ourselves, wonderful dividends come back. We may even gain friends and "relatives for life" whom we would never know if we did not get involved.

Carol chose the inner-city nonprofit medical clinic where she works because she is expected to give more there than standard medical care. Reflecting on her experience of listening to a despairing patient, she says, "A wonderful bond is established that makes life worth living for myself and for him!" She feels her calling is now much more meaningful than it was in her previous position.

After serving in this role for four years, she was visited by an old friend from a different city. They went to a lunch counter in the shabby neighborhood where Carol works. Some street people hang out there, and when she and her friend entered, many of them greeted her. A couple even gave her a hug. Her friend remarked with surprise, "These people all know you!" Carol responded, "Of course! They are my friends here."

She told me, "That's part of the joy and satisfaction I have gained. I have been making friends I would have never known." Her friendship represents love and hope to them. They naturally respond, filling a space in her life as friends who appreciate her compassionate and resourceful personality.

Healing

Sometimes surprising healing can come about for the person doing the caring. We all have wounds that either need healing or perhaps further attention from time to time.

Carl

Carl's life was disrupted early. His father was killed when Carl was only two months old. His mother was an alcoholic, and he was raised by grandparents. There were times when he did not see his mother for years.

As a teen he turned to alcohol and drugs. He didn't know what he was good for. Then while attending a community college, he took a class on death and dying. As a project for the class, he volunteered with the local hospice organization. About that same time he had been touched by the gospel and became a Christian. He wanted to change his way of living, but he found it particularly hard because he harbored anger and resentment over having been deprived of his parents. Carl says,

When I began to work with people who were dying, and with their families, I came in touch with other people's pain. I saw their confusion. I heard about the loneliness of a dying man who could not get his family to talk to him. I realized I was not the only person in the world with confusion and loneliness. I began to understand the human condition as it was experienced by others, and I felt the pain and struggle they endured. I began to see that God has pain too in loving his children. Here I was to help these people, and it was I that began to be healed.

Over a period of fifteen years, he has worked with 140 dying people and their families. As a hospice volunteer, he says that while he is giving assistance, he receives much more from them.

Mutuality Builds Self-Worth

Those of us who are healthy may forget how important our own usefulness is to us. Age, infirmity, or a disabling medical condition can halt or even end life's normal productive activity, assaulting one's sense of purpose and value. "What am I good for anymore?" is a common question.

Our work is one of our greatest sources of self-esteem, and contributing to other people's lives is a great source of satisfaction. When illness prevents a person from doing what they normally do, it amplifies their suffering. Let's look at ways we can expect more and encourage purposeful living. We can help empower a sufferer for meaningful and fulfilling activity.

Richard's Gift

We told part of Richard's story in the previous chapter. By the time he was in his forties, he had lived more than half his life with a chronic gastrointestinal disease for which he was hospitalized roughly twice a year. He had managed to finish a master's degree and taught some college classes in creative writing. Now, during years of unemployment, he made friends with other writers and poets. Those who knew him recognized he was an excellent teacher, a helpful critic, and a good poet. He had an encyclopedic knowledge, and was constantly educating himself in everything from art history and literary criticism to politics and baseball.

But because of his chronic illness, Richard had been unemployed more than ten years and lived on government disability benefits. He was often in pain and frequently suffered from insomnia.

During his late thirties, he had struggled with and eventually overcome drug dependency related to the medications for his illness. Much of his victory came through the help of Christian friends. At this time he returned to the church of his origin, his mother having been Catholic. He experienced a new birth and completed confirmation classes. This was a time of deep spiritual renewal and joy. Although physical ailments continued to bother him, he had new hope and energy. Richard began to write again. At his local parish he taught some classes, and his efforts were appreciated. He also learned to paint.

Eventually it occurred to him that although secular employers seemingly had no place for someone with his limitations, surely his mother church would. After researching a number of religious orders, he chose one that seemed appropriate and applied for membership. An interview was arranged, and the order's representatives seemed encouraging. Richard was gifted, and they appreciated his potential.

After a long wait, however, he was told that he did not qualify. Despite his spiritual readiness and his obvious intellectual gifts, the order could not accept financial responsibility for a person with his chronic medical problems. Richard was crushed as his hopes for a chance to belong and to serve were dashed. Once again he perceived he was being told he did not belong, was not needed, not wanted.

When Richard died at age fifty-three, I became custodian of his modest belongings, including his personal library. Among his books was one by Mother Teresa, *A Gift for God*. In it, Richard had underlined the following paragraph:

> God has identified himself with the hungry, the sick, the naked, the homeless; hunger not only for bread, but for love, for care, to be somebody to someone; nakedness, not of clothing only, but nakedness of that compassion that very few people give to the unknown; homelessness, not only just for a shelter made of stone, but that homelessness that comes from having no one to call your own.[15]

The important element Mother Teresa identified in suffering humanity is that of meaningful relationships, where people care about one another. In her order, the Missionaries of Charity, every caregiver is expected to offer more than just competent physical care to the sick and the dying. She taught them that quality care expresses love to every patient. Her order is known for the joy and love that is shown to everyone. In Calcutta, where Mother Teresa's work began, the nuns gather the destitute who die daily on the sidewalks or alleys of the city. She taught her order that these impoverished, soiled souls, abandoned by the society that passes them by, deserve respect and tenderness in their last days. So the nuns bring them into a place of loving care, as she puts it, "to die within sight of a loving face."[16]

Richard was my friend. Our relationship deepened as his illness and disability progressed. Our family helped him with physical needs, and we also included him in birthday parties and holidays at our home. But he was happiest when I sought his help. I was working toward an advanced degree, and he often asked about what I was reading or writing. Eventually he became my consultant and mentor. We had extended conversations exploring the more challenging areas I was struggling to master.

Richard was delighted when I began to give him my papers to read before I submitted them to my advisory committee. He had a keen mind and was an excellent critic and a great help to me. And he drew great satisfaction from seeing me achieve my goals. He became part of every success. Our productive relationship became one of the better chapters of his latter years. Richard had a gift to give. I received it, and we both were blessed.

Expect More Rather Than Less

We are too quick to expect less of senior citizens, especially when they have medical problems. One member of the caregiving team at a local church was getting up in years, and a series of new medical incidents cut his strength so much that it kept him at home. He could no longer get to meetings or accept assignments to visit others. However, he insisted that he could make a few phone calls each week to stay in contact with some of the "older" church members. He could not visit them in person, but he very much wanted to encourage them, particularly during difficult times. In this way, he continued to be a valuable team member.

By expecting and inviting such involvement, we are saying, "You have something to offer. There is someone you can help." We may not know for sure how this person can be of service to God or the community. But we can ask if there is some way they would like to help in serving others. People who are hurting are often the very ones most keenly sensitive to the needs of others with troubles.

Churches have come to recognize how important it is to offer disabled persons full access to facilities. But this is not enough. The next step is to provide full opportunity to get involved in ministry and give them an opportunity to develop and use their spiritual gifts. Our ministry to people with disabilities is too often limited to kindness. But in his book *Unconditional Love*, John Powell says that love, when fully developed, moves on from kindness to encouragement and challenge.[17] People need to be invited to grow in discipleship and be encouraged to use their gifts in service to God and their fellow human beings, even when they have a significant disability.

The sufferer may want to serve in some capacity despite his or her limitations. This is one way people regain a sense of value and purpose. Be ready to consider the practical dimensions of their ideas, and help them find ways to overcome obstacles. The Americans with Disabilities Act has put into legal form something we in the church ought to easily recognize: that disability in one area ought not cloud our perception of someone's valuable skills and abilities in other areas. We need to affirm their desire to serve in some way.[18]

Mutuality means we expect that everyone has something to give; there is opportunity for reciprocal giving and receiving. The apostle Paul used the phrase "love one another" dozens of times, and "encourage one another" as well (I Thessalonians 5:11). It was his way of promoting giving and receiving that nourishes healthy relationships. His call in Galatians 6:2 could be the motto for all caregiving: "Carry each other's burdens, and in this way you will fulfill the law of Christ." Mutual love and respect means that even in a ministry of caring, the giving goes both ways. Mutual respect restores and enriches relationships.

Be Ready to Receive

A sufferer's giving may take the form of something we described previously: gifts of stories, of wisdom, friendship, and healing. Or it may take some other unexpected, practical form that conveys appreciation and affection: a handmade object, a favorite book, or some other small item. Someone whose life is diminishing is often ready to let go of possessions. Accept their gift.

Only decline if you feel the gift is inappropriate. For instance, if it is valuable, consider how the family might view the matter. Also, if you are being compensated as a caregiver, pay attention to legal restrictions or employer regulations. If you must decline, do so graciously, and explain your reasoning to the giver. Perhaps suggest someone else who would be a better recipient. Declining a gift may seem to diminish its value and that of the giver. So as a general rule, be ready to receive.

The starting point is an attitude of expectation that the person has something to give you. But even deeper lies the bedrock knowledge that we are all engaged in a wonderful symphony of life whose rhythm is made up of giving and receiving. The most important things in our lives, whether material or relational, usually have been given to us, not grasped or earned in some transaction. They are gifts of love and affirmation, opportunities, or invitations—the kinds of things we ourselves find important and satisfying to give others. Whether they are tangible or immaterial, their value and meaning both to the giver and to the recipient makes them precious and unforgettable.

Studies of what gives happiness and satisfaction in life have repeatedly shown that unselfish acts of giving bring much greater happiness to people than receiving gifts.[19] Jesus said it simply: "It is more blessed to give than to receive"(Acts 20:35). "It is more blessed" most likely should be translated "It brings more happiness and satisfaction." The more we consciously participate in the symphony of mutual giving and receiving, the more meaningful and blessed life becomes.

Mutual Giving Is God's Way of Life

When we look at the gospel record, we can see that God is the originator and the most amazing demonstrator of mutual giving and receiving. Fourth-century theologian Athanasius pointed out that all three divine persons—Father, Son, and Holy Spirit—are deeply involved in the drama of salvation with a flow of interpersonal love. In our current era, theologian Ralph McGill writes, "Between the Father and the Son there exists a relationship of total and mutual self-giving."[20]

We see this in a few key gospel passages where we glimpse the interaction between God the Father and Jesus, his Son. The Holy Spirit also comes into the picture at Jesus's baptism.

> At that time Jesus came from Nazareth in Galilee and was baptized by John in the Jordan. Just as Jesus was coming up out of the water, he saw heaven being torn open and the Spirit descending on him like a dove. And a voice came from heaven: "You are my Son, whom I love; with you I am well pleased." (Mark 1:9–11)

The relationship of Father and Son is characterized here by a simple statement of affirmation and affection. The Father states Jesus is "my Son, whom I love." The Father is pleased with what Jesus is doing and how he is living his incarnated life. Besides, the mysterious presence of the Holy Spirit descends "like a dove," coming to rest on him and empower him. So there is a mutual involvement as the Son of God is affirmed and empowered to carry on his special assignment.

A similar affirmation occurs at Jesus's transfiguration in the presence of his three disciples Peter, James, and John.

> After six days Jesus took Peter, James and John with him and led them up a high mountain, where they were all alone. There he was transfigured before them. . . . Then a cloud appeared and covered them, and a voice came from the cloud: "This is my Son, whom I love. Listen to him!" (Mark 9:2, 7)

Jesus also spoke of his Father, from whom he had received all things, saying, "All that belongs to the Father is mine" (John 16:15). And he longed to return to his glory with the Father, of whom he spoke as his affectionate "Abba."

Even in Gethsemane. "'Abba , Father,' he said, 'everything is possible for you. Take this cup from me. Yet not what I will, but what you will'" (Mark 14:36).

Jesus poured out his heart in the garden, sharing his pain with his holy Father yet also willing to offer his obedience in the suffering he saw ahead. Our Trinitarian God—Father, Son, and Holy Spirit—

shows at the highest level what it means to be a person, to give and receive in mutual love, and to give of one's self.[21] Paul Fiddes, a contemporary thinker, puts it elegantly when he says that this dynamic giving between the Father and the Son is "the inner life of God, . . . the life that vitalizes God, not only in all his dealings with his creatures, but also eternally within himself."[22]

This understanding of godliness draws us way beyond simple moralizing or legalistic, false holiness. True godliness is all about self-giving in mutual love. As caregivers we are called to treat the person we are helping as a whole person who has something to give back. We give of ourselves. We hope and expect that the other person may offer his or her self to us. Our faith is in a God who, as three in one, reverberates with the power of mutual self-giving love and suffering. This defines for us a godly way of life.

Mutual Giving Is Godly Living

God's self-giving in the dynamic story of salvation draws us into the godly pattern of giving and receiving and a higher level of life—the life of God. Godliness means we are entering into that life as his hands and feet here on earth. This expression of salvation revolutionizes how we relate to people in all phases of life, including suffering.

In pain or suffering, we become vulnerable and needy, and if we are blessed to have someone care, a special bond develops between us. We respond with mutual giving and receiving, and joy is the result, paradoxical because it comes out of suffering. In turn, we become prepared to extend love and care when someone else is suffering. The cycle carries on in wider and wider circles, drawing God's children into his life.

Godly intimacy in caregiving lets us offer suffering people a quality of life rare in this world, characterized by unconditional love. We enter into others' pain by being with and serving them, and in so doing we discover something about ourselves. We become more complete. We sense a deep, mysterious connection to others and to God. Our sense of identity broadens and our souls expand as we include others in our world of personal concern.

♥

In a troubled and troubling world, intimacy is a powerful healing force. In God's own dramatic undertaking, he took on our human anguish through his Son and thus brought us salvation. "Surely he took up our pain and bore our suffering" (Isaiah 53:4). This is a story so deep that our words fumble to describe it. By bearing our burdens with love and passion, Jesus has proved to many a suffering human being that he is worthy of our trust and our love.

So too as caregivers we are engaged in renewing those whose faith is sorely tried, affirming that God is worthy of our trust and faithful in all circumstances. Love provides the greatest security and empowers sufferers to go through dreadful times with a greater measure of peace and confidence.

Love is the one currency that always adds to life. Relationships are what give meaning and purpose to all of life.

Conclusion

In this chapter we have considered how both the caregiver and the sufferer can offer precious gifts to each other. We must be alert to this remarkable dynamic for help and healing.*

There are more benefits to come. In the next chapter we will look at how serving someone in pain or trouble can draw us into a deeper relationship with God. Grace flows during times of shared suffering and makes it possible for a river of life-giving blessing to flow for both the sufferer and the caregiver.

---

*See appendix B, "Practicing Mutual Giving and Receiving," for hands-on ways to enhance mutuality in relationships.

FOR DISCUSSION OR PERSONAL REFLECTION

1 Which of the stories in this chapter has impacted your thinking or changed your mind about caregiving? Why?

2 When you encountered someone in need, did you discover they also had something to offer? Or did you only see weakness and impotence? How can you change your attitude?

3 If this chapter helped you to better understand the three persons of the triune God, how would you describe what you learned?

CHAPTER 5

Shared Suffering and Bonds of Healing Love

KEY POINTS IN THIS CHAPTER

1 When we share in someone's suffering, we bring new energy into the picture that can renew hope.

2 Sharing someone's suffering communicates love, promotes healing, and nurtures intimate bonds.

3 When we follow Jesus's pattern and willingly share in others' pain, we communicate the grace of God.

4 Intimate bonds formed through sharing pain give hope to the sufferer and reduce despair and darkness.

5 Maintaining healthy boundaries is essential to well-being for both the caregiver and the sufferer.

At the worst of times, when our defenses crumble, God often provides a friend who dares to come close to our side. And a miracle begins. This person becomes a catalyst that releases new energy and hope. A positive relationship can strengthen us to overcome the helplessness fostered by institutional or clinical care. Such empowerment helps us gain courage and renew our sense of autonomy.

The mutual giving and receiving in a caregiving relationship gives both persons a sense of involvement in something precious as their lives weave more closely together. We will look at some examples of how this happens. But before we do, let's consider what it means to share suffering.

How do we share in someone's suffering or trouble? It happens when we feel the discomfort of listening to disagreeable talk from a hurting person. We share in his or her suffering by waiting in silence when nothing adequate can be said. We share in their suffering when we help someone clean up their apartment, knowing it may soon return to its previous chaos. We share in the suffering of a guest recovering from surgery in our home when we clean the sheets after that person soils the bed in the middle of the night. Suffering comes to us in our discomfort, embarrassment, heartache, and frustrating work. But it is a price worth paying to fulfill our deeper purpose.

Daring Acts Renew Hope

People who go through extreme or harrowing experiences together, such as soldiers in a battle-tested platoon, often feel a strong bond of loyalty and affection for each other. So it is with some caregivers and those in whom they have invested much time and energy. People in these special circumstances often feel privileged to be trusted with someone's vulnerability as they share life's harder experiences. Time together takes on a deeper value, and a unique connection begins to grow.

Disappointments and frustration often leave people feeling raw, uncertain, and alienated. But connecting with others who really care and take time to know what's going on makes a world of difference. The deep bonds fostered in a time of heartache often come as a great surprise to the suffering person. At precisely the time when they are tempted to slip into despair, instead they experience a growing closeness to another person. That person's visits are eagerly awaited. Life does not seem so empty. And the positive energy generated can make a great difference in recovery.

This process can take many different forms. In the following pages we will unwrap it with real-life stories of how bonding and suffering with others reduced the power of otherwise devastating experiences.

Pamela

I met Pamela at the same HIV/AIDS hospice facility in Washington, DC, that I mentioned in chapter 3. Every resident is homeless and has entered the end stage of their disease. They are living the last chapter of life in a continual decline of capability and control over their own lives.

Pamela has a full work schedule as a news analyst in Washington, working for a foreign television company from one of our key allies. Her job no doubt provides her a comfortable living. Pamela is a young professional in a great career field. She is an attractive woman who appears to be in her thirties and could have a busy social life. But she has been volunteering at this hospice facility for the last couple years. What is going on here?

When she first heard of this place, Pamela told me, she would occasionally come to visit with the residents. The staff needed help with their tasks caring for these very sick men. She was drawn by the remarkable atmosphere of unconditional love demonstrated by the staff and observed how the residents responded with appreciation. A year or so before our interview, a personnel change created a gap in overnight staffing. The care manager approached her and told her about the shortage in their staffing. "Would you consider moving in with us for a while to help us cover the night time hours? You've gotten involved with our work and you know what happens here. You have shown us you care. What do you think?"

Pamela told me it did not take long to decide. The eagerness with which her heart responded surprised her. She moved into the home. Although she expected her stay to be only temporary, it became permanent. Together with a few other volunteers, she helps the staff provide a stable, home-like atmosphere where up to ten late-stage AIDS patients are lovingly cared for. Volunteers and staff take regular shifts. Pamela continues to work her day job and then comes "home" to this unique place of respite for desperate souls. Making the rounds to visit the residents, she catches up on how the day has gone for each one. And she serves them in whatever way they need help. Besides the evening rounds, emergencies occur during the night, such as cleaning up a patient with diarrhea or who cannot keep food down.

As I listened, amazed, to her tell me about her duties and her attitude, I thought of the price Pamela was paying to take part in this ministry. What could motivate someone with her qualities and career to take this on? Seeing my questioning expression, she explained how life has changed for her.

This has become the most precious time of my days and weeks. I am so glad I made the move. I have come to realize that my life and the sick person's are not so different. The difference between my health and their illness is not really that great. The time between my life and my death is not that much longer than the one whom I am serving, who may die this month. It is our giving and receiving that really makes life worth living. The openness and trust that develop between us here are precious. We are engaged in a mysterious life together, one in which vulnerability opens up windows I could never have imagined, joys I cannot express. I receive just as much as I give.

Pamela's sense of mutual vulnerability startled me:

We're not just here to give and 'do for' but to be available to receive, to receive from the other person. Every day and every hour is potent. Life here is on the edge and it is more iridescent, shining. You see things through their eyes you could have never realized on your own, at least not for a long time. I would not want to miss out on these experiences. I have so much joy in these encounters, I can't tell you.

I felt humbled, even embarrassed, that I had not expected this motivation. Pamela's attitude opened up windows of compassion I had not guessed existed. Yet she portrayed herself as nothing more than an average human being who had discovered something wonderful. Her attitude grew out of sharing the crucible of pain. Her experiences had yielded rich fruit of wisdom and peace. She was acquainted with grief. Yet it had not worn her out. Rather, it had given her a profound sense of joy and oneness with those whom she serves.

Pamela's testimony cast a bright, revealing light on my own attitude toward helping people. I realized I had not expected much more than to give my time and attention as a pastor, never anticipating I would be learning from those I helped or be blessed by their sharing with me. Pamela's experience clearly demonstrated how opportunities for caregiving can be life transforming for the caregiver.[23] These encounters and this way of life can be a source of deep satisfaction. Such results cannot be planned or guaranteed. But they grow like plants from well-watered soil as the caregiver applies skills invested with love. Godliness was demonstrated here in ways I could not forget. Pamela and others like her inspired me to share my own life more fully, the way God intended.

Sharing in Suffering Is Powerful

The dynamic process I want to describe takes us beyond the familiar steps of assisting someone with necessary tasks—not that I want to detract from the importance of meeting people's practical needs. Rather, I want to show how doing so can nourish something more profound. Choosing to share in someone's suffering

- communicates love,
- promotes healing of body and spirit, and
- nurtures connection and intimate bonds.

Life for the sufferer (*and* the caregiver) begins to take on meaning once again. Our connection to one another is what holds the precious fabric of life together.

Shared Suffering Communicates Love

Deliberately entering someone else's experience of suffering may be as simple as listening to them vent about a terrible job situation. Or it could require a bit more exertion, such as giving a ride to someone whose car is broken down and who needs to get to work on time. Maybe the person has been hit with an illness that threatens to unravel their finances. Listening to them can be a draining experience, and you yourself will feel frustration and desperation. But bearing that pain is your job.

Suffering forces us to recognize our limits, our vulnerability, our fragility. By coming close to others, especially to someone who suffers, we open ourselves up to pain. Becoming attached carries risks. We take in pain we might otherwise not have to experience. A suffering person knows this and will frequently say something to protect us, like, "Oh, no, I don't want you to do that for me. It's too much trouble for you." They don't want us to assume an unnecessary burden, one we could avoid if we chose. But that is why the caregiver's persistence in helping is a concrete statement of love.

Simply staying quietly by the side of a person in pain can have profound meaning. Author Louis Evely writes, "[Accepting] suffering in this spirit has redemptive power. And even a power which can be directed, it seems. People have been helped, supported, perhaps saved, because, on a given day, somebody prayed and suffered 'for them'—with them."[24]

Suffering willingly with someone becomes the ultimate language of love, communicating how precious we believe the sufferer is and how much we value our relationship with them. That is why God uses the language of suffering to show his love and encourages us to do the same. The key word is *willingly*.

Knowing God's story of intimate love and suffering can make a difference to those who feel no one has ever understood. It gives new words and meaning to people whose pain has seemed such that no words could express it. By choosing to become *intimate* with the human experience of suffering, God in Christ opened the way for a new bond of love.[25]

Jesus's words "I thirst" speak across the millennia for all who suffer. Jesus understands. We are following his lead when we deliberately enter into the scene of someone's suffering, opening ourselves to painful experiences we could avoid.

Howard

Howard was at our office to service the copy machine. I learned in conversation that he has served as an elder in his church. Our conversation revealed a thoughtful and committed man. I happened to comment that I was studying how to help people when they are suffering, and I asked him if being an elder had led him into any difficult encounters. He surprised me with his answer.

"I think we need to choose to embrace suffering," he said, explaining that he has often visited the hurting. On one occasion, the son of a church member had committed suicide. Howard went to visit the grieving family. Later, one of his church friends told him, "I knew I should go, but I just didn't know what to say." Howard continued, "I didn't know what to say, either. I just knew I should be there, and I went. It was terrible. But the grace of God gives us healing when we quietly wait for him."

Reflecting on Paul's statement in Colossians 1:24, Howard went on:

> Being a part of Christ's body, I believe we are called to suffer with others, something like it says, "I rejoice in my sufferings for your sake, and in my flesh I am completing what is lacking in Christ's afflictions for the sake of his body, that is, the church." I don't know if I have that all figured out. But maybe the suffering I take in because I'm with someone in pain is one part of God's plan to help bring salvation and healing to that person. I just believe we should really embrace the opportunities when we can willingly enter into suffering with someone.

This insightful layman has taken Paul's powerful theme of redemptive suffering and put it into action in his life. Howard considers suffering a part of his calling as a Christian.

Shared Suffering Promotes Healing

We communicate through more than words and ideas. Our actions convey great meaning as well. Taking time to help a disabled person eat a meal daily seems so simple; yet like the surface of the sea to a mariner, our actions, large and small, speak of depths and vast distances to one familiar with life. We communicate loyalty, love, tenderness, belonging, and value. Suffering for and with another person "is a language which penetrates more deeply than words."[26] It restores broken relationships and deepens bonds in ways nothing else can. The intimacy fostered by shared suffering is built upon mutual recognition of our vulnerabilities, our limits, our humility, and our shared grace.

"God proves his love for us in that while we still were sinners Christ died for us" (Romans 5:8 NRSV). We may have gotten a rotten deal, whether it is cancer, divorce, or unemployment. But when we realize that God himself has fully experienced alienation and desolation, we begin to be healed. In the same way, a broken relationship can be mended when one person reaches through the curtain of pain to touch the heart of someone who is hurting.

Lost and Found: A Father and Son Reconnect

I was in Maine staying in a remote cabin for a month of study and retreat. While driving down the highway, I saw, next to a house, a sign advertising firewood for sale. Needing to stock up, I pulled into the driveway. The owner, whom I will call John, was friendly and talkative, and he invited me in for a cup of coffee. Neither of us was in a hurry, and after a while he told me how he missed his adult son, whom he had not seen for fifteen years.

John had gotten divorced back then. His son, fourteen at the time, had rebuffed him in his early attempts to visit, due to the intense acrimony between John and his ex-wife. Eventually all communication broke down. John got no reply from his son to his letters and phone messages, and finally gave up in despair. A few years later, in order to take care of his aging mother, he left his job and moved several hundred miles to where I found him.

But John knew it was a terrible mistake to stop trying to communicate with his son. Then a year or so before our visit, he heard news through the maternal grandfather, with whom he still maintained a friendly relationship. John's son, now twenty-nine, was living on the West Coast and facing bad times. Underemployed and unable to afford an auto, the young man was beginning to despair of ever finding a real career and felt depressed.

John took the initiative to write a letter to his son. Soon he received a bitter reply: "Why are you writing now, after all this time? How can you say you really care about me? How could you leave and forget me when I was a kid?"

The letter was painful to read. His son had endured three or four stepfathers. There had never been a stable person to be a father to him. The young man was angry and disappointed with everyone who pretended to be a parent.

John wrote again. He reaffirmed his concern and acknowledged that his son had every reason to be hurt and angry. John tried to explain that he had learned a lot about himself over the years and regretted his mistakes. He invited his son to write back again with honesty. John told his son he would accept whatever feelings were expressed, painful and critical as they might be. The son responded again with language that was only slightly less harsh.

Their correspondence went on for several months. John finally urged his son to telephone collect anytime because he knew the boy's income was meager. And eventually the call came. It was an awkward conversation but a small step forward. As the months rolled on into the second year, occasional phone calls continued. John offered a modest amount of money so his son could obtain a used car. The young man also struggled with relationships, his sexuality, his poor career prospects, and the like. John offered counsel and encouragement.

Sometime into the second year of their contact, at the conclusion of a phone conversation, came words John thought he would never hear: "Dad, I want you to know I love you." John said it was one of the greatest days of his life.

He continued, "Now we have plans for my son to fly out here to see me for a week this summer. I told him to send me a picture of himself so I'll recognize him. I can't tell you how I'm looking forward to this visit."

Here I had stumbled upon a story of great pain and greater redemption. A man who had contributed to the wound of abandonment his son endured was able to muster the courage to attempt reconciliation. In the process he faced the anger and frustration his son felt. And the father began to bear his son's pain in a fresh way. He also shared some of his own pain with his son. These exchanges were terribly difficult, but John's love empowered him to persist. And that persistence, and John's willingness to listen to many painful words, became the catalyst for a wonderful breakthrough. A broken relationship was healed, and father and son are individually in the process of healing as well. Because they suffered together in a new intimacy, renewed trust and redeeming grace came into being.

Hospice and Healing

When we face losing something or someone and can do nothing to stop it, we are forced to recognize our limits. Our extreme vulnerability during a time of pain can become the opportunity for a breakthrough, whether like John's or in some other surprising way.

Illness and the threat of death are such occasions. Kevin, a hospice volunteer, explains that when he visits with families, their vulnerability allows him to become a catalyst for healing when a loved one is dying. He said:

> Many times, a person will tell me some of the troubles in the family, discord between adult children, and the like. Then I ask, "What would you like to do about it?" When requested, I have then brought people together and shared what was the concern. In many cases family members have learned things about one another they would never have known. Some have gathered around the dying parent, and longstanding wounds have been healed. Brothers and sisters have been reconciled. Families and individuals have received great peace and joy. This work is all about healing.

Shared Suffering Nurtures Intimate Bonds

Kristin is the nurse mentioned earlier who heads a nursing facility for homeless men who have been discharged from hospitals. They have nowhere to go, but they need further time for recuperation in a safe haven. Kristin says:

> Many of these men have lost everything—job, property, friends, family, their health, their privacy. The feelings of abandonment and deprivation are enormous. Vulnerability comes out. I have learned so much from these men. They have made me more aware, more than I would have ever learned otherwise, of how God is working in my life through people and circumstances. They have gotten beyond the illusion that we are really able to be in control of our own destiny, or our life circumstances. I have seen a sense of total abandonment into God's hands. With such deprivation, what is left? Only a vulnerable person.

Her words point to a particular dynamic that fosters depth in a relationship. When a suffering person loses more and more of the normal elements of life—possessions, appearance, health, autonomy, and so on—that person naturally feels vulnerable. In the midst of that vulnerability, a caring person brings an anchor of hope. Having a relationship of trust restores a modest but valuable source of stability.

Illness, mishaps, and turmoil in life can lead to deeper intimacy in marriage too, if people dare to open up. In their book *The Intimate Marriage*, Howard and Charlotte Clinebell write, "Crisis intimacy is the strength which stems from standing together against the buffeting of fate; standing together in the major and minor tragedies which are persistent threads in the cloth from which family life is woven."[27] One couple reported that suffering through the do-it-yourself experience of insulating their house together during their first year of marriage fostered a deeper bond of love. Many people I have interviewed were dealing with illness and death. But there too the movement in relationship described was toward deeper oneness.

Anna

Anna cared for her husband for almost two years during a debilitating illness. She quit her job when the seriousness of his illness became clear. She wanted to care for him and make the most of the time remaining while he could travel and enjoy a bit of life. When he needed home care, she would provide it. She would have it no other way.

Neither of them was, by nature, inclined to be talkative. Yet they became closer to each other during those months than at any other time in their long married life. It is hard to imagine that a couple's final weeks together could be their best time together. But this is exactly what Anna and others have told me.

Caregivers I interviewed frequently testified that those they have served sometimes told them things they had never talked about to anyone before. The responsive caregiver is often drawn into a surprising level of intimacy. Sometimes the bond that develops can bring an unexpected degree of heartache to the caregiver. But it can also bring joy and satisfaction. The suffering becomes fruitful rather than fruitless. When our defenses as caregivers melt away, we become open to receiving the gift of love, and bonds can form on deeper levels than ever before.

The Faithful Daughter

One middle-aged woman told about supporting her dying mother. The tale may seem macabre, but it is also a profound expression of love.

> My mother and I had many differences. During my teenage years and adult life, she often seemed to be self-centered and frequently complaining. My father had left her when I was a young adult. Other family members had little desire to share her company. My sister lived too far away. I was the one who was with her when she needed something. We visited often, even though many times it was not a pleasant experience.

When she became sick and needed more and more help, I made a decision. I felt that even though she often seemed unable to offer me the love I desired, I would do my utmost to make her last year or two better. I never regretted it. Sometimes I resisted the demands. Sometimes I said, "No, I can't." But to a large degree, I was there whenever she needed help or just needed a companion. She seldom said thanks. But her heart seemed to mellow as the weeks and months slowly passed. We talked very little about her prognosis. She didn't want to talk about it, and I didn't either. We both knew it was grim. Sometimes we played cards. Occasionally she was well enough to get out and do a little shopping.

As she grew weaker, I spent more and more of my time at her home. In fact, during the last two months, I simply moved in with her. I worked as little as possible and arranged for someone else to be with her a few hours at a time when I had to be gone.

During the last week, she often said, "Please don't leave me alone." I assured her that I would not leave. When the evening came in which I felt she could hardly live another day, I made a little supper for myself and she drank a few sips of water. Then she said in a familiar but weary voice, "Don't leave me alone." I slipped into bed beside her and put my arm around her. She went to sleep. I felt at peace. I knew there was no more to do. I prayed for her to have peace too. When I woke up a few hours later, she was no longer breathing. I had not left her alone. And I think she died at peace.

This woman overcame her own negative feelings and followed the better instincts of loyalty and unconditional love that she knew her mother needed at this stage of her life. Somehow the process of giving care and attending to her mother melted her own defenses and allowed her to venture farther than she ever expected. Ultimately her unconditional love yielded a harvest of wholeness and peace.

Intimate Bonds Communicate God's Grace

If shared suffering is so potent an instrument of love, we ought to make sure we recognize and embrace its opportunity. It allows us to live out Jesus's way of life, following his pattern for conveying God's grace.

As a caring friend, you may experience the pain of simply knowing and keeping someone's deepest secrets that they have shared with you. By your silence and by your tears, as well as by your actions, you may convey compassion that lightens another's load. Bearing another's burdens of frustration and impotence can help transform their attitude and bring about a new kind of empowerment. The best answer to their black hole of despair may be that someone like you boldly accompanies them into the fearful darkness.

This is exactly what Jesus did for us. He accepted the depth of suffering, the darkness of human failure and misery, and his act created our salvation. "Surely he has borne our infirmities and carried our diseases . . . and by his bruises we are healed" (Isaiah 53:4–5 NRSV). Likewise, our modest acts of selfless suffering can change lives and also open eyes to see Jesus in us.

Sharon

The mundane often becomes a medium for the profound. Sharon provides home care for sick and elderly people during times of decline, when they can no longer care for themselves without help. She comments:

> One thing you have to be ready for if you take care of someone who needs help is that there will sometimes be resistance before you get any payback in gratitude.
>
> One man I took care of was well over ninety years old but had lived independently all his life up until just recently. When I first came to work in his home, he seemed to fight me at every turn. He was angry and resentful of his situation. He needed help, and

yet, when I was hired by his family, he challenged everything I tried to do.

Finally one day I asked him if he wanted me to quit. He said, "Why?" I told him that I tried to do just what he wanted, and to do things the very best I could, but nothing seemed to please him. He almost cried. He asked me to stay and told me he really wanted me there.

After that turning point, we had so many good times together. He needed more and more help with personal things, but he never resented my help. He would test me with off-color jokes and everything. We became very close. He could talk to me about real things, funeral plans, hopes and fears. "You're almost like a wife to me," he once said. I know I was. I was wife, daughter, nurse, and doctor. He became so precious to me, as I did to him.

People like Sharon dare to live out what Psalm 23:4 promises: "Even though I walk through the darkest valley, I fear no evil; for you are with me" (NRSV). Bearing trouble together with people changes and deepens our relationships.

One pastor told me of a couple who had been joyfully expecting a baby until a diagnosis of Down Syndrome shattered their excitement. When they next met with the pastor, with whom they were only casually acquainted, they expressed their pain, frustration, and disappointment with God. Yet they felt God shared their pain.

The pastor heard them out and felt many of the same things. Their relationship was changed from a casual one to heartfelt closeness.

Sharing in suffering can gain us a friend and establish a relationship of confidence. For some people, few words need be spoken. For others, a verbal witness to God's grace may encourage and strengthen them—after one has *earned the right* to speak by showing love in action. The power of co-suffering opens people to hear the words of the gospel that we might not dare to speak before. Hearts connected by the intimacy of shared suffering can talk about the love of God in new ways. Bitterness can melt away when our words and actions become a window through which the sufferer sees our Lord Jesus, who was "a man of suffering and acquainted with infirmity" (Isaiah 53:3 NRSV). The power of Jesus's resurrection becomes more real when seen through the experience of suffering, and the promise of new life becomes more believable.

Jesus distinctly instructed his disciples to pursue a self-giving life-style and to expect suffering as a natural part of it. It is a deliberate choice: "If any want to become my followers, let them deny themselves and take up their cross and follow me. For those who want to save their life will lose it, and those who lose their life for my sake, and for the sake of the gospel, will save it. For what will it profit them to gain the whole world and forfeit their life?" (Mark 8:34–36 NRSV).

Jesus's words point to persecution and rejection. But to live one's life in Jesus's way also means giving up one's personal pleasure and comforts to share in the life of someone who is hurting. In this way we can bring redemptive power into our relationships and give up ourselves as we take up a "cross" we would not otherwise have to face. Sharing in someone's woes is clearly a form of intentional cross-bearing.

As heirs with Christ, we are part of the family of God, and we are the body of Christ. Our calling to enter situations of suffering out of love for others is consistent with our life in Christ. Paul's writings make this plain.

> I regard everything as loss because of the surpassing value of knowing Christ Jesus my Lord. For his sake I have suffered the loss of all things, and I regard them as rubbish, in order that I may gain Christ. . . . I want to know Christ and the power of his resurrection and the sharing of his sufferings by becoming like him in his death. (Philippians 3:8, 10 NRSV)

I am now rejoicing in my sufferings for your sake, and in my flesh I am completing what is lacking in Christ's afflictions for the sake of his body, that is, the church. (Colossians 1:24 NRSV)

Erika Schuchardt expresses her disappointment that Christian discussions wrestling with the problem of suffering frequently do not consider our practical calling to be human channels of God's love. In her view, these discussions miss the point when they do not consider the unique parallel between God's care for us and the practical support we can give people when they hurt. In order to make God's love real, she says, our theology must be clothed in the human behavior by which we bear suffering for one another.[28]

The New Testament clearly calls us to appreciate the value of suffering. As part of our participation in the body of Christ, it takes on greater meaning. Willingly endured, it is a privilege that confirms our identity. We can take joy in knowing it contributes to the fulfillment of God's salvation story. The intimate relationships that come about in times of shared pain become avenues of grace and effective ministry, bringing people closer together and closer to God.

Shared Vulnerability Promotes Hope and Healing

Suffering affects us in unexpected ways. It breaks our self-reliance and self-sufficiency—illusions on the surface of our lives that hide areas of weakness and disorder we don't want to face. Giving up the illusion of invulnerability opens us up for healing in the deeper parts of our lives.

When a hurting person becomes more transparent, sharing his or her feelings, fears, and hopes, it is an opportunity for changes in values and in relationships. Caregivers in tune with this change can respond with their own sensitivity and openness. They can honor the other person's intimate thoughts and honest feelings with reflective listening. And they can share their own painful emotions, such as "I ache for you. This must be very hard to bear." It is a time of shared vulnerability.

People who lower their protective barriers find new resources for healing. Deeper intimacy and trust promote growth; honest and open communication may reveal concerns never previously discussed. Perhaps the sufferer longs to heal broken relationships. Maybe they feel guilt over past failings. When the pain in one person meets up with love and pain in another, there is opportunity for wonderful healing.

On the other hand, sometimes a person withdraws into a fortress mentality, and there's no getting through to them. Sometimes a dying person responds with increasing withdrawal. Talk and touch get you nowhere; that person chooses to wall off the world.

But others will open up in ways they never have before. An attentive caregiver can make all the difference, so the sufferer can dare to move beyond the safety of their walls. In his book *Suffering: A Caregiver's Guide*, John Maes recounts the following story by the Reverend Doctor Mwalimu Imara.

> I was told that the patient, Miss Martin, was recovering from rather extensive abdominal surgery for cancer, and the more she healed the more demanding, abusive, foul mouthed and cantankerous she became. The chaplain's office was called in. . . .
>
> Through the patient daily ministry of pastoral care, this patient's story unfolded. She had been competent, successful, and increasingly lonely throughout her lifetime. When her serious (ultimately terminal) illness was discovered, she responded with incredible bitterness. But through careful spiritual direction and group work she was transformed into a woman who said to her group, "I have lived more in the past three months than I have during my whole life." Just like any major change in life, serious illness, with all its suffering, is an opportunity to evaluate, reconsider, and start in a new direction. This poignant story points out an important principle for caregivers to remember. That is, that growth can continue until the hour of death.[29]

Maintaining Healthy Boundaries

I have challenged you to go deep, to dare things that inevitably draw you into sharing someone's suffering. But there are risks you need to be aware of. You may find yourself intimately engaged in the realities of the sufferer's life. The bonds formed are a blessing, but they can also be hazardous. They can become bondage. You may feel trapped, confused, or overburdened; you may take on too much.

You are a caring person, but your caring can get you into trouble.

So, we need to consider some cautions. In chapter 2, the term *boundaries* was a metaphor for crossing over into painful territory as if it were an alien land. But the word has another application as well, commonly used to describe a key aspect of healthy human relationships.

Healthy boundaries are a natural and necessary part of keeping our lives in order and our identity clear. Boundaries delineate who you are and define the limits of your concerns, your freedoms, and your responsibilities. It is important to understand how such boundaries are involved in caregiving. They contribute to the well-being of both the caregiver and the sufferer when we practice the following.

Recognize the other person's freedom and rights. When we offer help, offer to pray, or any other action, the sufferer can say no. They may set limits on our interaction. A person may decide not to answer your questions or tell you about their problems. You may not have a very intimate encounter. A person preparing to leave this world sometimes will withdraw. This need not keep you from offering kindness and freedom.

Recognize the other person's responsibilities. If you find yourself rescuing someone or parenting them, protecting them from every crisis, you may be overperforming. If a hurting person is perennially calling on you for help, you need to know how to say no. Otherwise, you may prevent them from feeling the pain that is necessary to help them change and grow. If that person feels hurt, disappointed, or angry at your refusal, their feelings are their responsibility, not yours. You are not responsible for what has happened to them. Don't let their feelings provoke you into doing something just because you are uncomfortable.

Recognize your own rights, personal freedom, and limitations. When a needy person becomes dependent on you, calling on you for assistance again and again, you can say no for your own reasons. In 2 Corinthians 9:7, Paul gives guidelines for assisting other Christians in need. He writes, "Each of you should give what you have decided in your heart to give, not reluctantly or under compulsion, for God loves a cheerful giver." While the immediate application is to giving financially, it makes sense for any kind of caregiving. Once you've thought and prayed about what to give or do, stay with that limit. Keep in mind your commitment to your own mental health, your family, other obligations in your life, and your personal ability to help. Realize that you're not the only resource; other resources are also available to help.

Recognize your personal weaknesses. Caregivers with untended personal needs may slip into exploiting the trust placed in them. They can gain access to a vulnerable person's resources and misuse them for their own advantage. A sufferer may even realize what is happening but feel trapped by the care received, and even more vulnerable, powerless, and diminished. Caregivers must be vigilant of themselves.

Maintain your own boundaries in order to keep yourself living a healthy life. Caregivers need either a leader to supervise them or colleagues to hold them accountable. Times for reality checks help everyone keep a wholesome perspective. Pursue lifelong learning and a growing faith experience.*

---

*See appendices C and D for further help maintaining healthy boundaries, coaching toward practical choices, and nurturing the caregiver.

Accept responsibility for your own self-care. If you find yourself swayed by someone's anger or guilt messages, if you are prone to cave in at every request, then you have a spiritual and emotional problem that needs to be addressed. Seek guidance to gain control over your feelings. This is an opportunity to pursue your own spiritual and emotional growth.

Learning to examine our own motives, and understanding how to maintain healthy boundaries, is exceptionally difficult. That's why the further instruction and exercises in appendix C are important. I recommend you study them with a group or at least one other person.

Conclusion

Because we want to protect ourselves from pain, we're naturally hesitant about getting close to someone who is hurting or likely to die. But if you are willing to connect with those in trouble, you will discover the power of caregiving. Caring, listening, and bearing pain with someone are a potent act that changes things for the better. This daring attitude can communicate love, reduce pain, promote healing, and create precious bonds. The process can bring surprising joy and satisfaction. Connecting on a deep level helps us make sense of life.

Bonds forged in the furnace of suffering bring a new sense of salvation through relationships. It seems that what comforts us most is being connected—connected to someone who cares and connected to God in some unexplainable way. When we realize we are known and understood, and we in turn know the other person, our life deepens and takes on an identity beyond our own small self. Following Jesus's way, we fulfill our purpose by letting our identity grow to include others, and we gain peace in knowing we are connected through the deep streams of God's grace flowing through Jesus and through us.

This expanding sense of identity and belonging to others opens us to more fully recognize how we are also apprehended by the Great Other, that is, God. Faith thus takes hold of a new reality beyond all others. We glimpse for ourselves what the apostle Paul yearned for: "Now we see only a reflection as in a mirror; then we shall see face to face.Now I know in part; then I shall know fully, even as I am fully known" (1 Corinthians 13:12).

When we follow Jesus's pattern, we discover his presence in unexpected ways.

For Discussion or Personal Reflection

1 Think of an experience when someone extended themselves to help you in a time of trouble. How did that person take on unnecessary trouble or suffering for themselves?

2 On the other hand, if you have gone out of your way to help someone in a difficult spot, what kinds of pain or discomfort did you feel?

3 How would you say it makes sense that sharing someone's discomfort or suffering is a way for you to follow Jesus's pattern and fulfill his purposes? Describe how it feels to be Jesus's hands and feet?

CHAPTER 6

Discovering Jesus's Presence

KEY POINTS IN THIS CHAPTER

1 Sharing in someone's suffering imbues life with deeper meaning by giving us glimpses beyond the surface and insight into God's activity.

2 Caring activity creates intimate bonds that can transform lives and illuminate the presence of God in human intimacy.

3 Honestly expressing our pain to God can become an offering that leads to experiencing God suffering with us.

4 Some caregivers experience deep joy because they see each person as precious and find that serving them leads to greater wholeness for both.

5 When one's final days and hours are acknowledged openly, they can be transformed by grace and gratitude reflecting God's presence.

6 Those who serve with acts of mercy, immersed in caring for others, sometimes have surprising spiritual experiences of Jesus's presence.

I HOPE YOU WILL ENJOY SATISFYING NEW RELATIONSHIPS WITH some of the people you walk with through times of suffering. Most likely you will discover a deeper bond with a few special people, those you have come close to in difficult times. Your presence is a gift and generally appreciated by the sufferer.

But if you are a Jesus follower, you may envision a bigger picture and hope something more is going on. In this chapter I want to look at some ways God may show his involvement in what you are doing. He often surprises us with unexpected glimpses of something beyond ourselves. Like streams of sunlight that break through a cloudy sky, God gives encouraging signs of his presence. We may recognize God is involved when we

- feel we are in exactly the right place, bringing help and being the agents of God's love as Jesus's hands and feet.
- recognize God's presence in the person we are serving—God identifying himself with that person. ("Whatever you did for one of the least of these brothers and sisters of mine, you did for me" [Matthew 25:40]).
- realize that God in Christ Jesus has suffered, and is suffering, with us and with the person we are serving.

- get a glimpse or a revelation that we are standing on the edge of a deeper reality that lies beyond the mundane—a spiritual world of grace, love, and beauty.
- gain an insight, some wisdom that dawns on us or is given us by a person whose life is on a precipice of vulnerability.

We can learn to look beyond the everyday and beyond the pain to discern God using us for his purposes. We will find meaning we had not recognized before. Sometimes in a time of pain people discern and even celebrate Jesus's presence. There is no formula for this discernment, but I want to give you a sampling of others' experiences that connect with your calling, and mine, to care.

Jesus's Daring Entrance

Tragedy and misfortune disrupt a person's sense of order and stability. But an effective caregiver, entering where suffering and heartache reign, challenges their ruling power through his presence. Perhaps a whole family feels life has crumbled. This was the case when the man Jairus came and appealed to Jesus to come heal his daughter. While Jesus was en route, "someone came from the house of Jairus, the synagogue leader. 'Your daughter is dead,' he said. 'Don't bother the teacher anymore'" (Luke 8:49).

Could there be a more poignant expression of hopelessness? The mourners have already begun to wail, and grief fills the air when Jesus arrives at the home with Jairus. Yet Jesus does not hesitate to enter—and in doing so, he displaces grief with courage and hope. Jesus sees beyond the presence of death. "My child, get up!" he says. And she does.

Will *we* be daring? We want to be bold enough to enter someone's chaos without giving up our own sense of order and security. It is not easy. But sensing God's presence and his faithfulness can enable us to journey with that person into their valley. Sometimes, like Jesus, we will find ourselves walking amid wailing mourners. But when we realize we cannot do it on our own, we may sense him accompanying us. We can be signs of God's present hope in counterpoint to human despair.

This chapter will focus on how God reveals himself in the worst of times. You and I can be tuned in, looking for and expecting his presence to transform grief and pain.

Glimpses beyond the Surface

Hard circumstance, such as a dreaded diagnosis, can turn a person's whole world into colorless unreality. Everything seems like a gray blur, with darkness at the center of life. If we are with someone in that gray place, we can be pulled right into the maelstrom of defeat and despair. Our resources will seem quite inadequate. We can't fix the problem.

But just by offering a listening ear, a sympathetic heart, and a humble spirit, we can be of help.

Most people appreciate help in this humble form. The hurting person knows that no one else can fully understand their predicament. But amid their loneliness, a few special people can make God more tangible. Real caregivers bring God's presence with them, consciously or not. Some caregivers recognize this is their rare privilege.

Tom

Tom is a recovering drug and alcohol abuser. His experience helps him to be an effective volunteer peer counselor for others with addictions. He encourages them by sharing in their struggles to overcome their habits. Walking alongside them is not a dispassionate experience. He feels their frustration, their sense of failure when they fall away from recovery despite their best intentions.

But he also feels the deeper current of this drama. He says, "God allows me to feel their pain. Pain is a gift. It's a privilege for me to feel their pain." To feel their grief, their resentments, their self-loathing and frustration. Tom is walking with terribly hurting people, recognizing that this is a holy calling.

One privilege of a watchful caregiver is to observe the deepening of character in people enduring great troubles. A man or woman facing a life crisis may awaken to the importance of things long neglected. They proceed to sort out the meaning of things, weighing life's concerns differently than before and making remarkable choices. Endurance and character surface that might surprise that person's family.

The sufferer's highly focused thinking and conclusions may trouble those present. Wisdom is not always welcome. A person may recover from a life-threatening episode and make big changes in life priorities. On the other hand, sometimes a dying person wants to make plans and put things in order while the rest of the family does not want to deal with reality. The alert caregiver gets to see a miracle being played out. It may be necessary to stand in the gap, appreciating the mixed-up emotions of the grieving family while at the same time validating the concerns of the sufferer. The words of the apostle Paul become a reality, "knowing that suffering produces endurance, and endurance produces character, and character produces hope, and hope does not disappoint us, because God's love has been poured into our hearts through the Holy Spirit that has been given to us" (Romans 5:3–5 NRSV).

A Nurse Learns from Her Patients

You and I need to be ready to see beyond the surface and look for what God is doing or saying to us in the circumstance we face. A nurse who often works with very ill and impoverished people reflects on lessons she has learned.

They have helped me recognize illusions I have harbored. For instance, the illusion that we can control our life and its circumstances has been wiped away for them—and so this illusion has been taken away for me too. They have helped me realize how much I am dependent on God and other people with whom my life is inevitably woven. It's a humbling thought, but it does my soul good. We like to cling to the illusion that we are in control. But that's just our egotism, which God eventually must wipe away if we are to grow.

One attitude we caregivers must maintain is the readiness to learn. The circumstances we're serving in may be terribly disconcerting on the surface, but God is there as well. And we may learn something from the sufferer, from the situation, and ultimately from God.

The unique bonds formed amid suffering are much more than just another human phenomenon. Not only do they forge a deeper friendship but they can be a medium for grasping the deeper realities of life and meaning. They open doors to this wisdom, that *what really matters in life are our relationships.* Caregivers often come to recognize the more profound purposes of a relationship, be it husband and wife, friend and friend, or pastor and neighbor.

Brandon

Brandon is a pastor who has befriended a man in his thirties with multiple sclerosis. On the man's better days, he can get around with near normality. On other days he is miserable.

The man is not part of Brandon's church, but Brandon finds in him a stimulating friend. The man is often well enough to ride along with Brandon as he visits the distant hospitals that serve his rural community. Brandon says,

> One thing that really has made a difference, I'm sure, is that I have experienced some of the anger and frustration that this man has himself. He knows that when he voiced his complaints about God and life, I did not reject those feelings. Consequently we began to trust each other. There is a oneness and togetherness which has been good for both us. We have developed a deep bond.

As much as I did not want to accept it, I have become convinced that we are sometimes called to share in Christ's suffering as well as his joy. As this has worked out with my friend, I see that in severe illness the layers of superficiality often fall from those who suffer greatly. And so, I have the opportunity to see an intimate side of their life. I have come to believe that dealing on that level of life is what we were created for. When I serve those with severe illness I always sense that I have been closest to the essence of life.

This caregiver learned something from the unique experience of his friend, who was living nearer to the edge of life. Being close to him caused the pastor to peer over that edge and glimpse things that are mind bending. This special vantage point can be frightening, like peering into an abyss. But it can also be revelatory and beautiful. Like visitors gazing over the edge of the Grand Canyon, we may be shocked by the awful, dizzying depth yet at the same time stunned by the glory and wonder of the scene. Sharing in the life experience of someone walking close to the edge, we are privileged to get a glimpse of that landscape. Although we are one step removed from the experience, we can grasp some of the inner wrestling with fear and despair, the frustration tangled with hope, the tear-stained beauty of delicate, fragile life. We observe the believer "longing for a better country—a heavenly one. Therefore God is not ashamed to be called their God, for he has prepared a city for them" (Hebrews 11:16).

Discovering God's Presence in Intimacy

Sometimes everyday words can point to something rare and beautiful. In the following incident, an ordinary expression opened up a wonderful reality, and casual acquaintances became sisters of the heart.

Rachel

A woman in her thirties who belonged to Rachel's church became ill with cancer. Rachel had been casually acquainted with the woman and her husband through their church circle. She describes her experience this way:

> She was about my age, but we were never close. Then when I learned that she had cancer, I went to visit her. It was hard at first, probably in part because of my own inner fears. But I felt a sort of calling to befriend her in this difficult time. I began to be a regular visitor.
>
> She seldom talked about her fears. She tried to live her life almost as if nothing was happening. At first she said she didn't need any help. She wanted so much to remain independent. Eventually she agreed to let me go with her for chemotherapy treatments.
>
> You have to understand that she was not inclined to be expressive about affection. She was a `non-hugger,' if I may say so. It so happens that neither of us have brothers or sisters. After some months had passed, when she was quite weak, one day she greeted me: "Hello, Sis." It was her way of saying something profound had happened between us. It was a wonderful moment. After that day, she always called me "Sis," right up to the end. We had really bonded. I have never felt closer to anyone other than my husband. In spite of her reticence to talking about inner feelings and even about faith in God, I learned so much from her about love and about life. It was really a gift to me.

She changed my life. I had the sense of my being used as an extension of Jesus's hands and feet for her. After her death, I told her husband, "Thanks for letting me have her in my life."

Rachel told me she had the peculiar feeling near the end that she was not merely "doing something good" for this sister. She felt caught up in a story of God's mercy and grace, and privileged to have a small part in living out that story.

♥

As in Rachel's experience, a dying person may be profoundly moved by someone who is willing to form a friendship and become attached when it is clear they will soon be parted. This daring choice comes across as a wonderful sort of courage, courage to reach out even though doing so will ultimately bring pain to the caregiver. It is a Christ-like endeavor. In Rachel's case, her modest acts of loving care built a bridge, and the bridge grew into a heart connection, a relationship like that of sisters. Moreover, as a caregiver, Rachel saw her place in God's merciful scheme. Her viewpoint expanded with the satisfaction of being God's instrument.

Rachel experienced three God-given signs. One was an intimate bond with a suffering sister she had known only casually before. The second was the feeling of being Jesus's hands and feet serving her friend. The third was a perception of Jesus's presence with them, enduring the pain with them. Said Rachel, "I felt God weeping with us."

A different caregiver had a similar experience of God suffering with her. The words of Isaiah took on meaning like never before:

He was despised and rejected by others; a man of suffering and acquainted with infirmity; and as one from whom others hide their faces he was despised, and we held him of no account. Surely he has borne our infirmities and carried our diseases; yet we accounted him stricken, struck down by God, and afflicted. (Isaiah 53:3–4 NRSV)

Deepening of relationships cuts the power of pain. Even when someone is preparing to die, new relationships can occur, and they are potent connections. New linkages forged in the fire of despair are like anchors for the soul. The person who is willing to befriend us at the very time when death threatens us with separation is like an island of security in the sea of uncertainty. New connections birth meaning and hope. God becomes a vital reality.

An Offering of Pain to God

Not everyone experiences God's presence in a comforting way. Sometimes it seems God is silent or absent when we are disappointed with life. Despair gets the upper hand. On one of his more miserable days, Richard, whose story first appears in chapter 3, said to me, "I don't know anymore if there is a God. But if there is, I don't think he likes me."

Richard's example of being open, honest, and vulnerable in his relationship with God startled me at first. But as caregivers, we need to offer unconditional love by listening without judging when a sufferer feels led to spout complaints, to unload grim, angry, or frightened thoughts. A caregiver can encourage this kind of honesty. It is one more form of intimacy. Painful thoughts are no longer hidden but, rather, acknowledged out loud and consequently laid out before God.

Richard's story reflects the agony of having a dozen surgeries in twenty years. Again and again he was hospitalized. He seldom spoke to me with bitterness about his painful marathon. But he did struggle, and eventually he shared with me the following poem as his offering of pain to God.[30]

Bloodsweat

Gasp with fierceness
the thrust of knife
into gut.
Fight, breathe, fight
the fever, the raw
scraping pain.
Wires & tubes
blossom
from the bed.

Pain begins
the ruthless
search of the waters
of body & soul.

Come, gentle Jesus
nailed
to a wooden cross.
Be with me,
Jesus, in my agony.

"Bruised, divided, full of pain,"
You suffered
life and death
that I
in all this
might live.
Make my suffering
part
of your Passion.
Transform all agony
into Calvary.
Jesus, gentle brother,
bold with blood,
hear my cry,
my scream, take me
in your strong arms,
teach me,
even in bloodsweat,
to know the joy
of Calvary.

Elizabeth Elliot

Handing our pain and suffering over to God can yield unexpected results. When we are not honest about our negative thoughts, we may be blocking a full relationship with God. In Richard's case, his honesty led to a moving expression of his hope and faith in the crucified Jesus. It seems clear that our God is not intimidated by suffering nor offended by our painful words.

Elizabeth Elliot told of running totally dry of prayer when her second husband, Addison Leitch, contracted terminal cancer. Her first husband, missionary Jim Elliot, had been killed by tribal people in South America. Now, when she was about to lose Addison, a day came when there was nothing she could pray. She finally said to God, "I have nothing to offer you but my pain." She said God replied, "Then give me what you have."[31] In that intimate moment she offered up her pain, her grief, her disappointment. She realized in that experience that God accepts the broken heart.

It seems that when we open ourselves vulnerably to God, we may more likely feel the touch of the One who suffers with us.

Some Dare Speak of Joy

The rewards of caregiving are frequently described in terms of experiencing God in a deeper way. One is the perception, as Rachel described it, of being the hands and feet of Jesus in serving the hurting person. A second way is the exhilaration of recognizing Jesus in the person we are serving. This brings a deep joy in the privilege of serving him intimately. A spiritual experience like this enables some people to celebrate the presence of God's love even in the midst of suffering. Some even dare speak of joy.

Clarise

Clarise talks with wonder of discovering joy in serving people who are suffering. She previously was assigned to mission work in Africa by her religious order. Lately she has been serving in a small group home for indigent patients. She speaks of the inner needs of these people and how they touch her own. She tells about the unique intimacy that can develop when the normal defenses and masks we use are set aside.

In that time of service and openness, Clarise finds peaceful glimpses of life in the presence of the Divine. Here in her own words she shares her experience of joy in the midst of suffering.

> Nothing is worse than having a physical disease and then having the added isolation and rejection of others. That is why being here makes me so happy. It gives tremendous meaning to my

work. I feel the call to friendship at the heart of my desires. In that context I best understand what being a healing presence means. It gives me such a lot of joy! Life at this house has an intensity about it which is surely shaped by the fact that death is no stranger to us. Twelve men have died in the last twelve months. Life is short. Time is precious. Let's be as real as we can be. Love should be lavish. What are we saving it for, anyway?

I asked, "Isn't it painful to say goodbye after letting yourself become so attached in this way?" Clarise's reply demonstrates the paradox of suffering love.

Oh, yes. I mean, it's excruciating. But I wouldn't miss it for the world! It is transforming me. I've experienced profound love here, and that has made it all the more precious. I can't imagine doing anything else.

The rewards of serving in a Christ-like way include a unique joy that can only be understood by those who have experienced it. Loving acts that call for significant sacrifice bring people to the edge of their ability. Their consciousness gets stretched into another realm that melds pain and joy. Perhaps this is the kind of love and joy Jesus was describing when he said, "I have said these things to you so that my joy may be in you, and that your joy may be complete. This is my commandment, that you love one another as I have loved you" (John 15:11–12 NRSV).

Joy comes from the peculiar awareness of seeing beyond the painful sensation of the moment, or seeing in that moment something wonderful that is not apparent to others. The writer to the Hebrews calls us to look to Jesus, "the pioneer and perfecter of our faith, who for the sake of the joy that was set before him endured the cross, disregarding its shame, and has taken his seat at the right hand of the throne of God" (Hebrews 12:2 NRSV). At our distance, Clarise's comments about joy may seem to come from a strange, idealistic vantage point. But she is not alone in speaking this way. Another person who volunteers in the same home says, "I came to volunteer here because I could see the reality of something wonderful at work here. In the company of people motivated by faith, I recognized radical unconditional love. Even though I am often physically exhausted, I enjoy a deeper peace of mind than I ever anticipated. My heart sings."

Reports like this make it plain that joy erupts and blossoms in those special holy moments when we know we have been together in the depths. We are bonded to one another in the unspeakable dynamic of shared suffering. That moment, that day, becomes a gift from God worthy of our thanks.

Mother Teresa: Joy in His Presence

Mother Teresa's Missionaries of Charity are well known for the remarkable joy with which they do their work. Mother Teresa expressed her views on discipleship and suffering in simple yet profound language reminiscent of the apostle John. Two brief quotes say much:

We do it for Jesus, to Jesus and with Jesus.[32]

To show great love for God and our neighbor we need not do great things. It is how much love we put in the doing that makes our offering Something Beautiful for God.[33]

Joy is the unique hallmark of the Missionaries of Charity in Calcutta, India. Mother Teresa's order of Catholic sisters is founded on a deep spirituality that informs all they are taught to do and how to do it. When Malcolm Muggeridge went to Calcutta to prepare a documentary on the order, he expected to witness a peculiar kind of service to the dying performed by the sisters. He had heard that impoverished, dying people were collected from the streets of that city and brought into a home, where they were cared for in their last hours. He expected a story with unusual flavor, a story he could file for publication and then return home. But his life was changed by his visit. He came into close contact with both the suffering of those in need and the compassion of those who served them. He wrote about the sisters:

> Their life is tough and austere by worldly standards, certainly; yet I never met such delightful, happy women, or such an atmosphere of joy as they create. Mother Teresa, as she is fond of explaining, attaches the utmost importance to this joyousness. The poor, she says, deserve not just service and dedication, but also the joy that belongs to human love. This is what the Sisters give them abundantly.[34]

Mother Teresa explained that their work is, in part, a response to Jesus's parable describing the great judgment in Matthew 25.

> Then the king will say to those at his right hand, "Come, you that are blessed by my Father, inherit the kingdom prepared for you from the foundation of the world; for I was hungry and you gave me food, I was thirsty and you gave me something to drink, I was a stranger and you welcomed me, I was naked and you gave me clothing, I was sick and you took care of me, I was in prison and you visited me."
>
> Then the righteous will answer him, "Lord, when was it that we saw you hungry and gave you food, or thirsty and gave you something to drink? And when was it that we saw you a stranger and welcomed you, or naked and gave you clothing? And when was it that we saw you sick or in prison and visited you?"
>
> And the king will answer them, "Truly I tell you, just as you did it to one of the least of these who are members of my family, you did it to me." (vv. 34–40 NRSV)

Mother Teresa taught her followers to recognize that God has identified himself with the hungry, the sick, the naked, the homeless. This illustrates the intense spirituality that informs everything those in her order do.

The work we do is only our love for Jesus in action. And that action is our wholehearted and free service—the gift to the poorest of the poor—[and] to Christ in the distressing disguise of the poor.[35]

She explained how she was able to avoid being overwhelmed by the numbers of people in need and the weight of this burden. Her attitude demonstrated a truly contemplative approach to action—seeing God in the midst of the activity, which so many of us find hard to do.

I never look at the masses as my responsibility. I look at the individual. I can love only one person at a time. I can feed only one person at a time. Just one, one, one. You get closer to Christ by coming closer to each other. As Jesus said, "Whatever you do to the least of my brethren, you do to me."[36]

When suffering is shared and endured as a medium of love and as an avenue of intimacy with God, there are unforgettable joys in the midst of heartache. This is one of the lessons in a "school" most of us would choose to avoid. But then are we not missing out on some of the best of life? We can take steps to bring God's grace and love into moments that otherwise might slip away unfulfilled.

In Dying, Moments of Grace

One family told me how they experienced God's presence during the last days of their father's illness. Jane's husband was nearing the end of his endurance. He was being cared for in a nursing home after unsuccessful attempts to correct the heart condition that was now wearing him out. The family doctor informed her and their three adult children that although her husband was still talking lucidly, he most likely would not live beyond two or three days. The doctor was inclined to avoid telling his patient the full truth. But their pastor advocated a different course.

First of all, the pastor urged the man's wife and children to be open with the dying man. The pastor said, "You don't want there to be any barriers of confusion or mistrust between you in these last precious hours." They agreed. The dying man had been a college professor who was known for his candor and direct conversation. So they decided that he deserved to know the facts regarding his condition. His wife and one of the sons told the dying man how close he was to the end.

Then the pastor suggested a second step: the family could share in the sacrament of Holy Communion. When they asked the dying man if he would like that, the light of approval spread across his face in a moment. A few hours later, the two sons and daughter gathered with their mother, their father, and the pastor in the man's small room. The pastor led them in a brief reading from the Bible and prayers. They shared the bread and cup together. The man's wife and children offered their own words of love to him, and he responded in kind. He glowed with a satisfaction and peace that inspired them all. Joy and peace surrounded them as they felt embraced by the grace of God together.

In her later years, Jane often talked of how the last days of her husband were transformed into a time of blessed sharing and joy. This act of worship had become a profound expression of their shared faith, and their sense of God's presence brought deep joy.

In a different time and place, a woman who happened to be a nurse was caring for her husband at home. He had lived a long and fruitful life in mission and ministry. But now his cancer was much advanced, and they welcomed few visitors. It was the concluding episode of a months-long decline. The woman told me how she and her husband had celebrated God's presence on the day he died.

There had been times when her husband shared happy memories and they talked freely with visitors. At other times, this highly educated and deeply committed believer's conversation ranged into the heartfelt questions of life and death. "Why, after all these years of faith, do I have to endure this pain? What am I good for?"

The time came when the wife's medical experience alerted her that the end was very near. For three days her husband's signs had pointed to it. On the third day his breathing was labored. The TV was on in the bedroom, but she decided that the one thing he did not need to hear was the noon news. He had always loved Handel's *Messiah*. She put that music on the player in the bedroom. During the next two hours, its glorious expression of the gospel moved with them through this holy time. While the "Hallelujah Chorus" was ringing out, he breathed his last. She said, "What more precious moment could we have to remember?"

Once again, an occasion of heartache was transformed by the light and love of God's presence.

Celebrating Jesus's Surprising Presence

The interplay between pain and joy is peculiar and counterintuitive. We naturally try to shield ourselves from grief and pain. But by letting ourselves be pulled into the stream of God's movement among us, we get beyond what comes naturally. A supernatural impulse draws us beyond the risks and discomforts.

By nature we are risk avoiders, but God is the ultimate risk taker and has given us a brilliant example in the suffering and crucifixion of Jesus. Avoidance is not our calling; immersion in loving risk is our calling. Choosing to be there for someone can be exactly the avenue to joy and fulfillment. We may meet God in an unexpected way. One woman told me how she encountered God in spite of her attitude.

Kathleen

Kathleen resented having to work on Thursday evening of Holy Week. She worked at a small rehabilitation facility for homeless men who had been hospitalized and treated but were not yet well enough to return to life in the community.

Maundy Thursday was one of Kathleen's favorite times to be at worship. She never missed the occasion. Communion on this night was always special. But this year the schedule called for her to be on duty. She resented the way things had worked out and how unfair it all seemed.

As the evening wore on she busied herself with its mundane tasks. Not many patients needed attention. But one man requested help. He asked her, "Could you please cut my toe nails?" So she sat down to do the job. He was appreciative, but she was quiet and not in the mood for conversation.

As she was finishing, though, something occurred to her—the picture of Jesus washing his disciples' feet on that last evening. His words from the gospel of Matthew seemed to burn in her heart: "Whatever you did for one of the least of these brothers and sisters of mine, you did for me." She was almost startled by the realization of his presence in the room and momentarily ashamed of the self-centered attitude she had harbored. But that quickly passed as the whole experience transformed into one of awe and pleasure. She thanked the man for asking for her help. For her it had become a holy moment, and a very Holy Thursday.

Discovering God's presence in the mundane moments of life and service can transform disappointment and grief. But we will miss the transformation unless we watch expectantly and humbly for the Holy One's presence. God mysteriously works through the adverse, through pain, turmoil, and suffering, to draw us to him and toward a fuller understanding of life's meaning.

Preparing Ourselves to Encounter Jesus

So how do we discover the presence of Jesus in uncomfortable moments? We cannot make a spiritual encounter happen at our convenience. However, we can mold our consciousness to be ready for the opportunity. We can train ourselves to watch for God's surprising presence.

We must immerse ourselves in the Bible. Reading the Gospels helps us absorb the influence of Jesus. In this way we also let the attitudes of people who encountered Jesus seep into our own being.

Most important, we can ask Jesus to be in us. With his courage in us, we gladly practice going toward pain, purposely stepping into situations where suffering threatens to dominate the scene. In conversing with someone who hurts, our own discomfort may pull us off track. We want to get away. We want to change the subject. But instead, we must seek to fully engage with the other person.

Finally, we need to arm ourselves with prayer. Before every visit, we need to pray that God will empower us to see beyond the disorderly, the discomforting, the pain or blood that can disturb our senses. We can pray that we will see a child of God who is in deep trouble, a precious one whom God loves. We can pray for courage and love to motivate us, pray that we may love that person, no matter how difficult it may seem. Praying for love is more important than praying that we will "know what to say."

Bonhoeffer's Last Months

Dietrich Bonhoeffer was imprisoned during World War II under suspicion of his involvement in an anti-Hitler plot. During that time he had many conversations with others whose lives, like his, were hanging by a thread. He frequently shared a humble worship service with the other prisoners, and they broke bread together in the name of Jesus.

Eight months before he was executed, Bonhoeffer wrote to his friend Eberhard Bethge: "It is certain that our joy is hidden in suffering, and our life in death; it is certain that in all this we are in a fellowship that sustains us. In Jesus God has said Yes and Amen to it all, and that Yes and Amen is the firm ground on which we stand."[37]

"Our joy is hidden in suffering"—but it is not at all apparent that suffering is the place where we will find joy. This seeming contradiction points to a mysterious paradox. It is true there are times when we need to withdraw from pain to survive, physically or emotionally.

Some Eastern religions even encourage us to disengage from this world by denying all passions for life. But Jesus's way calls us into the pain of others. Paul the apostle tells us, "Bear one another's burdens, and so fulfill the law of Christ" (Galatians 6:2 RSV). We can choose to be near the pain of others. We can give precious time to be alongside someone whose hours are dreadfully long. We can choose to be secondary sufferers when we endure the frustrations and disappointments of someone with whom we walk a while.

Following this compassionate and painful path, we approach the center of the cross. We are with Jesus in his pain, his compassion for all the chaos of humanity, and we are in the good fellowship of the cross. Our bond with Jesus and with others is deepened, and it is our joy to be with him in his great purpose: to heal what is broken. He welcomes us all into his love, and as we share that love with others in pain, his deeper joy flows through it all.

Some questions will linger. Why is there so much discord and pain in life? What happens to faith under pressure? But please know that you have already found the most important part of the answer by obeying Jesus's call to walk with someone through a difficult valley. These are precious opportunities. It is our privilege to accompany our Lord as he walks with someone who is hurting.

Conclusion

Our Lord Jesus demonstrates that suffering with another person is the deepest channel for communicating love and is a potent way through which we come to know one another more fully. God has chosen this path to reveal himself and his love to us. "God was in Christ, reconciling the world to himself" (2 Corinthians 5:19 NLT). Likewise, when we choose to serve someone and share some of their suffering, we are given an opportunity to "to know [Christ] . . . and the fellowship of his sufferings" (Philippians 3:10 NKJV). These are occasions we will not want to miss, and when they occur, they are never forgotten.

FOR DISCUSSION OR PERSONAL REFLECTION

1 Have you ever had the feeling that Jesus was near, or have you been surprised by God's presence in some situation? Describe what happened.

2 How do you feel about expressing disappointment to God or questioning his ways? If you've ever done something like that, what happened?

3 When you have come near to someone else's chaos, did it rattle your sense of order and security, or could you manage your feelings? What happened and why? Did you just try to get away?

4 If we pray for God's presence and sense his faithfulness, we can walk into the valley with someone. How might you need to grow in spiritual sensitivity?

CHAPTER 7

What Happens to Faith under Pressure

KEY POINTS IN THIS CHAPTER

1 While going through trouble and suffering, believers find God bringing them to deeper levels of faith and trust in him.

2 Recognizing the limits of our understanding, and of our ability to change others or our circumstances, can bring us greater peace.

3 We make sense of suffering in different ways as we dive more deeply into our trusting adventure with God.

SERVING PEOPLE IN TIMES OF SUFFERING, SHARING IN THEIR TROU-
ble, often leads to occasions you will treasure. You may witness inner
healing and profound joy. But those who suffer also raise troublesome questions—Why is this happening to me? What is this suffering all about?—and you will often be drawn into them.

Some people endure suffering with patience; others, with agonizing bewilderment. When you or I face serious trouble, we are likely
to pray, "Help me get through this." We need strength to endure.
And in the Bible we find prayers like this one in the first chapter of
Colossians:

> Since the day we heard about you, we have not stopped praying
> for you. We continually ask God to fill you with the knowledge
> of his will through all the wisdom and understanding that the
> Spirit gives. . . . being strengthened with all power according to
> his glorious might so that you may have great endurance and
> patience. (vv. 9, 11)

Endurance and perseverance are virtues the Bible teaches us to
pray for. And people are often given more strength than they expect,
enduring great burdens with surprising confidence. Likewise, helpers and caregivers often receive strength seemingly beyond their
own capacity to serve and uphold those suffering some of life's worst

circumstances. And often something else happens as well—something more, unexpected, a blessing, spiritual outcomes they did not anticipate.

Stories from the Edge: Spiritual Outcomes

I have heard remarkable stories of unforeseen blessings in the face of pain—sometimes a whole series of events. It may begin with a fearful diagnosis, or an accident, or a family member's addiction. Trouble leads to more trouble; steps forward meet with frustrating setbacks or further grief. But then, most often as the person nears the end of their story, their face takes on a new, positive expression, a sort of visionary attitude. And they recount some remarkable experience that led them to insight, spiritual growth, and renewed faith.

Diane's Mother Stays Too Long

Diane's mother came for a two-week visit. She lived near Diane's sister in a distant state, and consequently Diane only saw her about once a year for short visits. Her mother was becoming irritable as she aged and had developed some limitations that made her feel frustrated. Her visit was going well enough, but Diane realized she was looking forward to her mother's leaving in a few days to go back home.

Then her mother fell and broke her hip and had emergency surgery to mend the bones. Recovery required physical therapy and time to recover her strength. Time Diane had not foreseen. After a couple weeks at a rehabilitation center, her mother came back to Diane's home. She continued her recovery with outpatient therapy sessions and was making good progress. But after a couple weeks, something went wrong. She needed more medical attention to address the issue. When she was sent home again, her ability to manage for herself was diminished. Diane had to attend to her needs and at the same time challenge her to do the exercises to regain full mobility. Her mother was frustrated and often complained. They were together almost all the time.

Being daughter, nurse, and therapy coach was a conflicting and stressful set of roles for Diane. The weeks were filled with follow-up appointments and sometimes long days. Diane's faith was being tested, she felt. She prayed frequently for endurance and patience, especially when her mother was cranky.

Diane got away for short periods for shopping and other personal chores. But this was not the summer she had planned. Her husband was supportive, but he was busy running the family business. Diane and her mother played cards. They watched TV together. Sometimes they reminisced about the good times long past. Occasionally they had some laughs. And sprinkled in it all was her mom's frustration and occasional outbursts about things that could not be changed.

The summer weeks slipped by. Eventually Diane's mother was able to return to her home across the country. As Diane told me how the summer ended, her expression changed. She said, "Although my mother was hard to live with, often unreasonable and argumentative, I know now that those three months turned out to be a time of deeper intimacy. We experienced a closeness we never had before. At the beginning I was hoping I could just survive the unexpected extension of her visit. But by the end I was deeply enriched by our relationship. I would not want to have missed that experience for anything."

The unexpected turn of events imparted something to Diane. She could treasure the relationship with her mom, and it would be richer from now on, however short or long the time would be.

Reflection

Although the unexpected events were stressful, both Diane and her mother were blessed by the length and intimacy of the visit. Diane's faith deepened as she began to recognize God's providence in the matter. Her prayers for endurance were answered in unexpected ways. Enduring challenges together with her mother became a blessing. Their bond was deepened as they met those challenges together. God enabled Diane to love her mother more fully.

Doug Faces the Unknown

Doug first experienced cancer in his midforties. This unexpected threat to his life required surgery followed by chemotherapy. After several months he recovered well enough to go back to work at his trade, although cautiously, since he still felt weak and limited. He was beginning to feel normal again about two years later when he began to notice a persistent pain in his back. He did not at first associate it with his previous cancer since it was in a completely different locale. But it was the cancer, showing up in a new site, metastasized in his upper vertebrae.

This was a shock. Doug accepted the surgeon's urgent recommendation for surgery, followed once again by chemotherapy. Recovery this time took over a year, but eventually Doug began to feel nearly normal, though with less stamina. He considered restarting his business but hesitated, fearing a relapse if he was not yet ready.

During his long recovery time, Doug was deeply moved by all the efforts of friends to raise money to help with his expenses. Besides this, a large number of people constantly offered their encouragement, support, and prayers on his behalf. Feeling grateful and wanting to do something for others himself, he returned to doing volunteer work with disadvantaged people. He felt a passionate concern for those in need, the homeless, and people in trouble. He also volunteered as a tutor, assisting students who needed extra help at the alternative high school.

Three years later Doug experienced another occurrence similar to the second. But this episode was even more frightening. His previous surgeon declined to operate because he felt the bone structure was too damaged to be repaired. They consulted a university hospital, where the new surgeon told Doug his spinal column might suffer permanent damage and he might never walk again. However, the high-risk surgery was successful, and with therapy, Doug began to regain his mobility. He would have to relearn how to walk. After three weeks he came home in a wheelchair. Soon he was walking with a cane, a grin on his face. He was gaining ground, and he relished every opportunity to be with friends at his church. Life was difficult. But Doug appreciated every step and every day.

Doug had assumed each surgery and treatment would be the last, but the cancer returned. It would be no surprise if this series of life-threatening events had worn his faith to tatters. Instead, his faith moved through questioning and deepened. As he described it, his first bout with cancer raised the basic question, Will I be all right? And he trusted that God would take care of him.

When the cancer reappeared, he began to ask, "What is God trying to teach me? What am I supposed to be learning from this?" The earlier question whether he could trust that God would heal him lingered, but a new depth of faith became prominent. He began to see his volunteer work as God's gift to him. He found meaning and purpose that made his days worth living.

Before his illness, Doug thought he could make plans for a long future with the assurance of a person his age. Now he knew there was a level of uncertainty in life for him. He wanted very much to live to see his daughter graduate and go on into adult life. But uncertainty colored every vision of his possible future. He learned that he could live from day to day and year to year, trusting that God would give him whatever he needed to live faithfully. At times he wanted to ask God why he had the cancer. But, he said, "I could just as well say, Why not me?"

The next couple years after our interview did not go well. The cancer returned twice more, and finally Doug lost any possibility for healing. At fifty-two he was dying after ten years of cancer, surgeries, and treatments. Hope renewed was always followed by a new recurrence, each time worse than before. Doug accepted this outcome and arranged for hospice care. He was deeply disappointed, but his faith and character continued to shine.

During one of my visits, just a few weeks before his death, Doug and I played guitars and sang together. His rich voice blessed me as we sang gospel tunes and old folk music.

At one point, he said to me, "You know, I don't have a lot of time, but I just hope that I can bless one person in some way every day I have left." He did that. And after he died, another acquaintance of his posted online the following:

> Recently someone told me how sorry he was that Doug had lost his battle to cancer. That statement jolted me. Doug did not lose any battle! No matter how many times it came back or how many surgeries he went through, he would stand back up and go on caring about others. He always asked about others with genuine concern and whether there was anything he could do. He volunteered in any capacity his health would allow to serve other people through the homeless shelter or other local ministries. He never turned his back on any youth he could help as a school volunteer. He never let cancer get in the way of loving his family.
>
> He never allowed cancer to take him to a point of questioning his faith in his personal Savior Jesus Christ. He never said "I give up!" He stood up to cancer and did what was needed. Any soldier on a battle field who does this is rightly called a hero. Well that was Doug. Even in hospice he never gave up. So I say He did not lose a battle to cancer, but won victory through Jesus Christ.

Reflection

Doug did not lose his faith, but rather learned to live more vulnerably, aware of God's grace. He accepted the unknowns that face all human beings. His suffering led him into an honest dialogue with God and more passionate service to others. Doug never gave up being a disciple of Jesus who blessed others.

Diving Deeper

What is going on in people like Diane and Doug? They are going deeper in their faith, experiencing levels not previously known. Distress seems to work on their faith like the pressure that creates a diamond deep in the earth.

When we want to help people enduring painful situations, we may be surprised by the questions they ask and the answers they receive. We will often find they are living in a different reality than ours. Their life journeys have included different valleys and heights. As a result, not everyone is living at the same level of faith, and not everyone will ask the same questions as you or I. Unique influences and a myriad of experiences have shaped each of us and nurtured our faith. Let's look at another story, one with a long arc of time.

Elizabeth the Sage

I first met Elizabeth when she was in her early seventies. She lived only a block away, and during the roughly twenty years I had the privilege of knowing her, we had many conversations. A vigorous woman, she had traveled widely and was a lively communicator. She also drove frequently in challenging Detroit traffic to visit relatives there.

Elizabeth had won several awards for her photography and was comfortable with technology, so when our church conducted a local work camp to fix up homes in need of repair, she offered to video record the progress each day. She circulated among the various work sites, capturing scenes, and at end of the week she edited the material into an eight-to-ten-minute presentation to be seen Sunday morning.

Elizabeth kept three portraits prominently displayed in her living room. One was her late husband; the other two were young people, a girl about eleven or twelve years old and a young man in his twenties. When I asked about them, Elizabeth let out a sigh and proceeded to tell me their stories.

She and her husband, Marvin, enjoyed an active life in their early marriage, and both had jobs. But they had no children, so eventually they decided to adopt. First they received a boy, and later, the girl, each of them only about a year old when adopted. They were eager learners and grew to be happy, busy children.

But when the daughter was about twelve, she was diagnosed with leukemia. Elizabeth and Marvin sought the best treatment available, but it was unsuccessful, and their daughter died in her first year as a teenager, at age thirteen. Elizabeth sighed again. "We loved her so, but that disease just took her away from us."

She went on to describe their son. "He was a really smart kid. He got through high school with good grades and got his engineering degree. But then, all of a sudden, when he was twenty-seven, he had a heart attack, and we lost him, too."

I was struck by the matter-of-fact way she told this sad tale. But her words were also weighted with a weary voice, just above a sigh. "We just couldn't believe it when we lost both of those wonderful kids."

Then she related quickly how she and Marvin had just gotten to their thirty-fifth wedding anniversary when he became ill and died shortly after. Elizabeth had been alone about fifteen years when I met her.

When I asked her how those trials had changed her, she said, "Well, you know, I couldn't just quit living. But I was mighty disappointed with how God had let things work out. I do have good friends, and God has allowed me to have a long life and a good place to live."

Being part of the community in a small town was good for Elizabeth. She was living an active life despite the fact that, as she put it, "when I turned seventy, things started to fall apart." She persisted in exercising and bowling every week for years until she was eighty-nine. And for quite a stretch in her eighties, she carried out the tedious process of making video copies of Sunday services every week for homebound church members. One time she said to me, with that gravelly drawl of hers, "Well, I guess the Lord has plenty for me to do yet, so I'm happy to be a part of the family God gave me, our church."

Reflection

In spite of searing losses, Elizabeth found healing being among God's people, and a meaningful life using her special talents to serve

God and his children. Her trust in God was deepened as he provided encouragement through her church. Elizabeth's questions remained, but they became less troublesome as she apprehended new reasons for living and serving with vigor.

Gerald and His Son

Gerald has been a successful professional and entrepreneur. He runs his life and his business with integrity and manages both well. But he has a son whose life has often been off the rails. The son has often lived irresponsibly, seemingly by the opposite of his father's values. There have been several women in the son's life, and children born from those relationships.

Alcohol and drugs have also been a part of the scene. Gerald has rescued his son more than once from a life-threatening overdose. Sometimes his son has tried to turn over a new leaf, but again and again he has turned back to his addictions and away from his father. Though he lives in a nearby town and now seems to be living a more stable life, the son remains distant and cool to his father, who has helped him recover from a number of disastrous situations over the years.

Gerald says, "I guess I have learned that I cannot make his life better. I have learned to let go of worrying about him or trying to rescue him. I have had to let go. I have backed off and tried to stay away from giving him advice or help. Since then, I have seen some people come into his life who are a good influence in ways that I had not expected and that I could not be for him."

God has revealed to Gerald that his son must solve his own problems without him. God has provided avenues for his son to grow and manage his life. Gerald has learned to let God take over, and now he has more peace of mind. It is a different answer to his prayers than he expected.

Reflection

Gerald has learned the limits of his own ability to change someone's life. His faith has been challenged over many years as he tried to be a faithful father and help his son. Now he has come to trust God as his Father in heaven in a way that has given him a greater measure of peace.

Recognizing Our Limits

One of the foundation rocks for peace of mind is knowing our limits. Both Elizabeth and Gerald have come to recognize that there are things they cannot change. They have each faced painful circumstances beyond their power to make go away. This is a form of wisdom, knowing what we can do and what we cannot, and then choosing not to fight a battle of worry or fruitless regret. Reinhold Niebuhr's well-known "Serenity Prayer" expresses this wisdom:

> God, grant me serenity to accept the things I cannot change, courage to change the things I can, and wisdom to know the difference.

Brian and Judy: Deep Loss, Deeper Love

Brian and Judy were both raised in homes where Christian faith was prominent. Both attended Christian schools. They first met at a church event for young adults, were married a year later, and had three children. The family enjoyed the outdoors, and the lake cabin Brian and Judy built was a source of pride and contentment. The two were close emotionally, and Brian says he doesn't know how he could have gotten through life without Judy. A tender, mild-mannered woman, she has been a great comfort when he's had down times or stress at work. Brian says, "I've cried on her shoulder more than once."

Brian had a serious digestive disorder at age fifty-one which led to surgery and several weeks of difficult, painful recovery. He learned to pray a lot during that year, while he worried that he would never fully recover. Then at fifty-three, just two years later, he had to have quadruple bypass surgery. He's very cognizant of his own mortality.

About the time both of them were in their late fifties, Judy began to experience odd lapses of concentration. She had taught third grade for years, but now their adult daughter noticed Judy was having trouble calculating grades, and the daughter occasionally helped Judy with that. But in another year or so it became clear Judy's problems were growing, and she retired from teaching. Brian himself had now reached retirement age as well.

They sought medical help for Judy, but the results were inconclusive. Over the next two years she exhibited new levels of confusion, and serious problems arose. She would start the car but could not figure out how to drive it. Diagnostic tests finally confirmed early-onset Alzheimer's.

Brian and Judy both experienced frustration and irritation when some new loss occurred. Brian attended an Alzheimer support group and studied books to help him cope and "know what to expect in coming years." Looking back, he berated himself for insensitivity and failure to recognize what was happening when some new loss occurred. "I should have known. But you just expect things to stay stable for a while. In her case, new things occurred every year, and sometimes more rapidly."

By her sixty-fifth birthday, Judy needed help dressing and bathing. Attending to normal chores was becoming impossible. Brian did all the housework and spent his time managing her needs. She began to have toilet problems. He frequently had to give her a shower three times a day in order to clean up. He realized it was not only cognitive lapses occurring, but she also had less and less control of her body.

Reflecting on this stage of their journey, Brian said that all of his life he had an aversion to hospitals, sick people, and health problems. But as his wife's needs accumulated, he found he could help her with the most intimate, and sometimes most distressing, messes without feeling repulsed. In fact, he felt "comfortable" going with her through these difficult exercises of patience. He had to help her with eating and everything else for her hygiene needs.

Brian said he never felt upset with Judy, but he occasionally experienced moody frustration when things occurred at a very inconvenient time. Did he ever begin to feel sorry for himself, I asked. No, he said, he didn't have those feelings. His great sense of compassion and empathy drew him away from his own self-concern.

By this time Judy could not express much in the way of love anymore, but her mild manner and gentle personality never changed. As her decline progressed more rapidly, Brian and his family finally decided she needed professional care. He was encouraged when he found a home where two of her former third-grade students worked. They remembered her fondly and were pleased to serve her needs. Their attitude helped enhance the warm, homey environment of the care facility. Brian was thankful to God for this great blessing.

Six months later, in midwinter, there was a new and sudden loss. The beloved family cottage Brian and Judy had built on the lake was destroyed by fire while Brian was away. The loss was complete. But when asked about it, Brian responded that the cottage was a small loss compared to losing Judy to the decline of Alzheimer's. He would have readily given up the cottage and endured that loss if it meant he could have had his dear Judy back with him. The two losses did not compare. Insurance would make it possible to replace the cottage, but nothing could replace Judy.

Several months after the fire, Brian reflected on the saga of recent years. He said, "I thank God every day for her. She is a real gift to me. Her tenderness has always been there for me. Her personality has not changed. She still is sweet and dear, even when she doesn't know who I am."

Reflecting on his earlier aversion to hospitals and patient care, he said he never felt that way about Judy's needs. He never missed an opportunity to be with her, even when she was unaware who he was. Brian pondered, "Maybe it has made me a better person." Early in their life together, they thought love was all the things they enjoyed, the romance, the adventure of living and working together. But now those were gone. "So why do I love this person now? She can't give me much of anything anymore. But I love her all the more. I guess now I really know what love is."

About a year after the cottage burned, Judy came to the end of her journey. The year following her death, Brian and I visited again. The past couple years had been distressful and yet profoundly meaning-ful for him. He was still finishing the inside of his rebuilt cottage. He was as consistent as ever at worship, and he also read spiritual writings. "Yes, it's been a year already," he said. "But I still miss her every day." He has no regrets about how much his love cost him toward the end of Judy's life.

Reflection

Brian's faith in God and his faithfulness to his wife were severely tested. But God has revealed to him how these difficult times have worked out to change him for the better. Even in the midst of great loss and pain, love has thrived. He has a deeper sense of wonder and amazement at how the love of God has worked through him and blessed both him and his wife.

My Children, O My Children

Few if any concerns grip us more fiercely than danger to our family and children. The following accounts demonstrate how a mother's or father's passionate desire for their children to flourish also opens the parent up to profound heartache. Protecting and caring for one's family is a deep and blessed commitment. When these goals are dashed by tragic events, and prayers seem to go unanswered, God still nurtures the soul amid the deepest sorrows.

Paul's Trials of Endurance

After four successful years in the Air Force, Paul responded to a job opening for a corrections officer at the county jail. He was consid-ering a career in law enforcement, and he was hired. His military experience had taught him to follow procedures precisely, and that training transferred well to his new job. His job transition went well.

During his first year on the job, a woman and her boyfriend were both serving six-month sentences for obtaining prescription pain drugs under false pretenses. They were not to communicate with each other while in jail. But Paul discovered they were violating this rule by leaving notes for each other in a library book, and they were duly penalized.

After their release, rumors circulated that she had bragged to friends that she might accuse Paul of molesting her in jail and could make a lot of money from a law suit. Paul's friends on the force all knew it was a lie, and Paul was not worried. He had done nothing wrong. But a couple months later, in February, the former prisoner filed her complaint. Paul was reassigned to a different position while an investigation was conducted. He expected the matter to clear up quickly.

Three months later things began to tumble down on him. In spite of this woman's doubtful past and previous deception, the prosecutor charged Paul with criminal sexual conduct. He was put on leave without pay. Reflecting on it later, Paul says, "I was shocked. I was only twenty-three; I was young and naive. I believed in the justice system." He was a responsible husband and the father of two children. He had been a faithful employee and looked forward to a career in law enforcement. But now the system had turned against him. How could this happen?

He hired a skilled defense attorney, knowing it would cost a lot of money. Worse yet, all contact with his fellow officers stopped. No one called. Contact with the sheriff's office came only by mail. Paul was suddenly a nonperson.

But he had no time for self-pity. He had no job and desperately needed income. He found work in late-night stocking at a big-box store in a nearby town, where he would have little contact with the public. His whole life was turned upside down.

During the next year and a half, the legal bills rolled in monthly.

Paul and his wife decided to sell their house to raise money, and his parents invited them to move in with them. As the dreadful months dragged on, things grew more difficult. Everyone in the family lived with constant tension, and occasional bickering broke out. Paul knew he might be going to jail. He was caught in an irresistible flow of events and felt responsible that his whole family was suffering because of his career choice. He felt depressed, alienated, and angry, abused by the very justice system he had worked to uphold.

But Paul was buoyed by his father's attitude. His dad, Mike, said to him, "We will pay the bills. We will use every resource we have, every credit card, whatever we have to do." This was not an easy commitment since they were not wealthy except in love and loyalty.

Paul's pastor, who was near retirement, and the pastor's successor at the church were both supportive and encouraging. Otherwise, precious few people reached out to Paul. In this desert of alienation, his father became a great source of faith, stability, and support. He believed in Paul. He even said, "We will sell our house too if we have to. We're going to get through this." His father's faith helped renew Paul's own faith.

Paul was angry with his accuser during the first month or so and hated her for wrecking his life. But that began to change. With his father's encouragement, he prayed through those emotions. He began to feel sorry for her instead. He came to realize that she was a person without a foundation like the one he had been given. She desperately sought satisfaction in life through falsehood, drugs, and crime.

During the second year, the prosecutor offered a plea bargain twice. The first bargain would have reduced the charge to fourth-degree criminal sexual conduct, a high misdemeanor. The second, a month before the trial date, was an offer for Paul to plea malfeasance of duty. But Paul was not interested in pleading guilty to anything, and he said no both times. Either option would have wrecked his future as an officer. Paul stuck to his integrity. The prosecution's case might be weak, but Paul and his lawyer still needed to prepare for a difficult trial in January. The unknown hung over his life.

For weeks, Paul's attorney coached him. The trial opened with a grueling day of jury selection, with each potential juror indicating whether or not they knew Paul. The trial itself turned out to be a giant farce and collapsed quickly. When the accuser took the stand, she gave new and contradictory testimony. By the next morning the case was dismissed.

Paul felt strangely undone. All his energy had been focused on a defense that was not needed. His lawyer's firm encouraged him to sue the county and the prosecutor. But Paul declined. He wanted to go back to work as a law enforcement officer and resurrect his integrity.

So it was over, and he was restored and reimbursed for lost wages. But he had lost almost two years of his life. The stress had been indescribable, and eventually his marriage came apart.

When I asked Paul what happened to his faith in this marathon of disappointments, he mentioned several things. His trust in God deepened as he observed his father's steady faith and firm commitment to see the family's time of testing through to the end. He saw his father's composure in the face of chaos while other family members were often in panic.

Paul said he knew he was being tested. He had taken for granted the security his family and his faith had given him. It was a revelation to him that in spite of God's love, life could throw terrible things at us; that "bad things do happen to good people," and we only get through them by trusting in God without expecting instant relief.

Paul simply wanted to pursue his career, to be faithful to his calling and to God.

Ten years later, while Paul was on patrol, terrible news came that his two daughters, aged fourteen and seventeen, were badly injured when their car was struck broadside by another. The younger girl's injuries were not life threatening. But the older one was being transported to a regional trauma center.

Paul was devastated. Doctors at the trauma center told him that in cases of people whose upper vertebrae were crushed like his daughter's, 98 percent do not survive. The staff expected her to die.

Their manner seemed abrupt, lacking in empathy. Paul was cut to the heart for his daughter. Never before had he felt such raw despair and helplessness. His sorrow was too much for words. Alone by her bedside, he prayed with desperate tears; he pleaded with God not to let her slip away. If God would let him keep her, he told the Lord, then whatever her condition turned out to be, he would gladly take care of her.

On the fourth day a neurosurgeon explained, with great compassion, that he had implanted a titanium support to stabilize the vertebrae. The girl's life still hung in the balance. At this point, Paul fixed his mind on one goal: to get her to the state university research hospital. Despite little encouragement from the present hospital staff, he persisted, and ten days later she was transported to the new hospital.

The staff there were encouraging. They conveyed a sense of calm confidence. They did not promise an ideal outcome, but they offered a step-by-step treatment plan. Over the next few weeks they worked the plan, and though the results didn't come fast, they did come. Weeks and months of therapy brought slow but steady progress.

At the time of my interview with Paul, four years after his daughter's accident, she had achieved a level of independence, living in her own home with daily helpers. She has permanent limitations but continues therapy three times a week.

Paul's second story has, like the first, been a long journey of faith and hope. Paul was immensely grateful for the miracle of his daughter's recovery. He takes pride in her accomplishment, and he gives God the credit for her being alive when all the indications were against her survival. He said, "The Lord gave her to me." Once again he reflected on life's uncertainty—and blamed no one.

Reflection

Paul believes life is too difficult and complex to blame God for things that go wrong. He says God has continued to refine him and make him a better person, a man of deeper faith, ready to face the rest of life with a profound trust in God. He knows he is a man of many faults. But he is a man on a journey to become what God intends him to be.

David and Rosalie: Losses Doubled

David and Rosalie had four children. They farmed, and both also held other jobs to supplement their income. Life was relatively stable as the kids were progressing through school, and everyone was involved in the local 4H club. Rosalie was an active member of a local church; David says he was a believer but attended infrequently. After graduating from high school, their oldest son, Chuck, decided job prospects for him would be better in New Jersey where Rosalie's sister, his aunt, lived.

On October 1 the next year, he called to tell his parents he had been diagnosed with cancer. What he had thought was just a persistent back ache was caused by a life-threatening cancer. Within days, Rosalie and his youngest sister drove to New Jersey, where Chuck's surgery was performed to remove the main tumor.

But there was more bad news. The cancer was a particularly aggressive type and had already metastasized in other parts of his body. A treatment plan began, with chemotherapy each day for a week; during that time, Chuck was an inpatient at a hospital near his home in New Jersey. He felt miserable most of the time and could not keep food down. He spent the remaining three weeks of the month at the home of his girl friend's parents. David or Rosalie traveled to be with their son whenever chemotherapy was being administered.

The months went by, filled with treatment, respite, and more treatment. Sometimes after a week of treatment the doctors expressed hope for his healing and said, "We think two or three more treatments will take care of it." But then Chuck's white blood cell count would drop so low that the next treatment was delayed. The tumors that had shrunk noticeably then quickly regrew.

After several months the doctors said his liver was being damaged by the chemotherapy and surgery would now be a better route. They aimed to remove all the lymph nodes containing cancer around the heart and liver to give him a better chance of recovery. However, they warned that he was very weak and the surgery would be difficult. The family gathered for the vigil. After hours of waiting, the surgeon told them sadly that he had not been able to remove all the cancerous tissue.

The family began searching for other options. In September, after almost a year of treatment, they contacted Memorial Sloan-Kettering Cancer Center in New York City. There they could use heavy doses of chemotherapy followed by bone marrow transplant using material harvested the previous year. In a frank conversation by phone, Rosalie asked the specialist who would supervise Chuck's treatment what his chances of recovery really were. The doctor said, "About 10 percent." Following that, she says, she went off to cry by herself.

After considerable hassle with his insurance carrier, Chuck was transferred to New York City, and the treatments were carried out the whole month of October. The trips by Rosalie, David, and other family members shifted to the expensive Manhattan environment. They were thankful when free housing at a church-sponsored facility became available. This took some worry out of the picture, but the other expenses were still draining their resources.

One night at home, worried about all the expenses soaking up their resources, Rosalie was pondering a Bible reading when, she said, she heard a voice saying, "I will supply all your needs." And again: "*All* your needs." She says this promise was fulfilled. Again and again, church and community support helped, and David and Rosalie made their own resources stretch. They both kept working the extra jobs. Somehow, they never lacked for what was needed.

But the ordeal went on. By December, fourteen months after the initial diagnosis, Chuck's condition continued to waver.

About this time, Rosalie wrote him a letter to express her love for him and also to convey the gospel to help clarify his faith. Then she had a conversation with him to make sure he understood that he was not likely to live much longer. She said, "The promise that I hung on to was 'Do not fear, for I am with you. Do not be afraid, for I am your God. I will strengthen and help you. I will uphold you with my righteous right hand.' Isaiah 41:10."

The treatment plan proceeded, but Chuck grew weaker. In March, after a year and a half of therapy, his mother and father were by his side when he unexpectedly experienced a wrenching convulsion. They tried to help him, but it was the end. And thus they endured the terrible grief of losing their son.

Both of them describe it as a shock, even though they had been through the whole long saga. David said, "I just couldn't believe it. He was only twenty-two. He had his whole life ahead of him. And now he was gone."

They made arrangements. They were comforted by the expressions of support and help. And they were flooded with visits, hugs, and greetings, though some were less than helpful. David says, "You know, when people say, 'Well, he's in a better place now,' it really doesn't help one bit. He's gone, and it hurts." Rosalie says, "But what does mean something is their presence, their hugs, the tears in their eyes. Those things are comforting."

We were already friends when these events occurred. Revisiting them many years later, I asked how the experience changed them. Rosalie said, "You have the choice to get bitter or get better." Her spiritual depth still keeps her in good humor. David, on the other hand said, "You don't get a choice about whether these things happen." He would like to ask God, Why? But he went on to say the ordeal has helped him have compassion for others in what they are going through. He admits he did not have much sympathy or empathy for people in trouble before his loss. "I would probably be out playing golf or taking care of my own things rather than stopping in to see some old man who can hardly see or hear or talk. But I know people all around us have problems, and I go see some of them, especially the old ones who don't have much family around."

♥

David and Rosalie's tragic journey was not over. While their younger son and older daughter had moved along into adult life smoothly, Karena, their younger daughter, had not. A perky, good-looking young woman, she was a restless risk taker.

About four years after Chuck died, Karena, just eighteen, had a child out of wedlock. This was especially distressing because the father did not want to take any responsibility for the child. Karena's future was going to be difficult. But with her parents' help, she held a job and began to raise her child.

When her girl was around five years old, Karena developed a painful condition that she treated with acetaminophen. Eventually she made the mistake of taking the drug in such quantities that it damaged her liver. She needed a transplant; without one, she would soon die.

Karena entered the Cleveland Clinic to wait for a donor. Once again the family received help from friends, churches, and others— it was welcome, but the funds didn't come close to the cost of the life-saving process.

Six weeks later, a liver became available, and the transplant was successful. Karena returned home and began recovering her strength. Life started to take on more normal dimensions the next couple years. David and Rosalie had hopes for the new boyfriend Karena had found.

But events were colliding. The antirejection drugs sometimes made Karena miserable. Then, although two years had passed, she received an unresolved bill for $30,000 for the transplant surgery. It was sent in error; the costs were being covered through a payment plan in combination with a charitable source. But Karena got the bill anyway. And it came when she was having a falling out with her boyfriend. Perhaps one of these things was the last straw. She was twenty-five years old, but life was not working out for her.

One afternoon she returned home from work feeling depressed. Later that day, while the granddaughter was staying with Rosalie after school, David stopped by at Karena's house. He sensed something was wrong. The dog was in the house but not Karena. David went to see if she was in the backyard. What he found was unbearable. Karena had killed herself with a shotgun.

"No—not again!" David recounted his words through tears. His and Rosalie's misery could not be put into words.

Over the next days of benumbed grief, hundreds of people expressed their support and love. There were the words, the hugs, the service. The ending of endings.

Twenty years later, we talked about this agonizing period. Rosalie mentioned Paul's statement in 2 Corinthians 1:3–5:

> Praise be to the God and Father of our Lord Jesus Christ, the Father of compassion and the God of all comfort, who comforts us in all our troubles, so that we can comfort those in any trouble with the comfort we ourselves have received from God. For just as the sufferings of Christ flow over into our lives, so also through Christ our comfort overflows. (NIV 1984)

She applies that to herself and David. The comfort God has given them equips them to offer comfort to others. "There's a story in everybody's life that you may not know," she said. "So I can't feel sorry for myself. All I can do is let God lead me to be a blessing by sympathy and compassion, doing what I can to help others who are in need."

David said, "Yes, you want to ask God 'Why?' and there's no answer. I guess we'll find out answers later on. But for me, it came down to, you've got to go on living. And you don't want to be like some old sourpuss who thinks that they have it the worst. Everybody's got their troubles. You come to realize that theirs may not be the same as yours, but theirs are just as real and what they need is for somebody to care, to come and be with them.

"Oh, I didn't used to go to church much. I still don't agree with everything the preacher says, but now I want to go to church, because I figure that God has led us through this stuff, and I need God. I want to help others. And I do it any practical way I can. Sometimes it's just cutting wood for a neighbor who needs fuel and can't buy it. So I guess it's softened my heart some—to notice what people need and not turn away from them, even if they are not very nice people or they have some bad habits. They are people God loves just as much as he loves us."

Rosalie said that in spite of it all, she has experienced what is really unexplainable: the peace she had when Chuck died, and then again when Karena died. "It is really 'the peace that passes all understanding.' You can't understand it. But you can have it."

We looked at some family pictures and exchanged hugs, and then I left. David and Rosalie's testimony was a wonderful gift to me. Through their great losses and heartache, somehow the grace of God prevailed in their lives.

Reflection

God has helped David and Rosalie notice and care about other people's troubles and needs. Both of them grasp a bigger picture: how God works in their lives and has given them comfort that they can share with others. They have come to a spiritual place where they accept life with "the peace of God, which transcends all understanding" (Philippians 4:7).

My Initial Observations

Considering the variety of painful problems these people endured, I was surprised that none seemed to have come to the precipice of giving up on God, losing their faith or settling into an angry sullen attitude. God had worked in each of these people to create something unexpected. Even if there was a passing phase of resentment or anger, none mentioned it. In fact, when I questioned, "Did you ever feel angry and let down by God?" they uniformly responded with something like, "No, but I was puzzled and confused at times." Almost all said they had grown closer to God as they learned to lean on him more fully.

These sufferers indicated that the most important outcome was some kind of spiritual growth. Some grew deeper in faith, expressing it as trusting God more profoundly for everything. Most have greater compassion for other people in trouble and show it in practical acts of mercy and assistance. Some have seen God deepen their love for a family member through very difficult times. All seem to accept the uncertainties of life with a greater sense of calm and wholeness, experiencing God's incomprehensible but very real peace. To faithful believers, God gives an unexpected gift of revelation, a wisdom that could come no other way. A gift gained only through suffering.

I would not pretend that this small sample of people's stories is a scientific basis for what to expect from any believer in time of suffering. However, among all the people I have known and interviewed, those here have endured some of the worst pain I can imagine. And the outcomes are remarkably similar: some kind of deepening faith and devotion to serving others.

Kintsukuroi is the Japanese art of repairing broken pottery with lacquer mixed with powdered gold, silver, or platinum. Kintsokuroi treats breakage and repair as part of the history of an object. The broken places gleam with precious metals.

Similarly, we can often see the beauty of a person developed, with new luster, through their trying experiences.

Yet during the process, we cannot escape a tension. We all want to make sense of what is happening. Life has to mean something. Even when the meaning is shattered by horrible events, we do not stop searching. We may be tempted to take the route Job's wife urged upon him: "Curse God and die!" But we are likelier to take Job's path and remain in conversation with God, seeking to trust him through it all. The conversation may have some raw spots, but the people I interviewed kept believing and looking for God to work all things together for good. (See Romans 8:28.)

For the caregiver, it is most important to be aware of transitional times when pain is interacting with the process of healing. Sufferers need time and space to voice complaints. Richard, who penned the powerful poem "Bloodsweat" near the end of his life (see chapter 6), had several darker periods earlier. During one of those times he said to me, "I don't know anymore if there is a God. But if there is, I don't think he likes me!" Yet his faith and his conversation with God moved on to something positive, even when he was immersed in a sea of pain.

As wise caregivers, we will avoid responding to uncomfortable statements like Richard's with our favorite easy solutions, which only serve to make *us* feel better. Besides giving time for a sufferer to go through phases of faith and doubt or stages of grief, we need to pay attention to how different levels of faith may be exhibited in the process of healing. Maturing or deepening faith is likely to lead to different conversations and a yearning for different answers at different times. Let's explore the ways distinct levels of faith appear on a journey toward wholeness.

Making Sense of Suffering

If you are serving someone who is in trouble, you will often be drawn into the deep questions a sufferer asks. How they are answered or endured depends on each person's faith journey.

We enter life with the innocence and hopefulness of children. As we grow older, our expectations become more realistic. But questions have a relentless way of reshaping themselves when we are confronted with the unhappy realities of life. Some people will endure these prickly questions but never voice them. Others will ask them out loud. And we too will hear discomforting questions pressing inside us if we spend time helping others navigate painful times.

Questions arise because we are confronted with the discord, the opposites of life. Suffering presents us with strain between life at its best and at its worst. At times we will be caught between conflicting emotions:

Whole, capable	vs.	Broken, incapacitated
Empowered	vs.	Enfeebled
Celebrating	vs.	Sorrowing
God is good	vs.	Where is God? Or, God is bad
God is able	vs.	God is not able to manage
God is awesome	vs.	God is awful
Togetherness	vs.	Isolation
Life is good	vs.	Life is terrible

As caregivers we need to not fear the pain in questions that arise. Sometimes the questions arise from the sufferer; at other times, from a secondary sufferer—a husband or wife, son or daughter, who feels the pain of someone they deeply love. We too, as caregivers, can become weary with the weight building inside. We search for meaning. We think, "I don't understand why there is so much suffering. Why does it have to be this way?"

Accepting the Struggle of Faith

This chapter is not about doubt. It is about faith. The questions sufferers ask, and that we ourselves ask, lie within the bigger arena of a relationship with God. When that is big enough to include a conversation in which painful thoughts can emerge, then we can move forward in faith, helping both others and ourselves.

Emotional stages like shock, denial, guilt, anger, depression, and resolution are reactions to important losses in life. They are important but relatively short-lived emotional states if we are healthy enough to progress through them and not get stuck. What we want to consider here is the deeper structure of one's faith.

The levels of faith we are about to describe are more like a series of residences where we live for years or maybe decades. For this reason, people will also approach the challenge of understanding suffering in various ways that reflect their particular depth of faith. When we understand this multilayered picture, we can better assist those who hurt in their journey toward wholeness.

Whether we suffer firsthand or, as caregivers, we enter the pain of those who do, we are like Jacob: we become one who wrestles with God, working out our faith in fear and trembling. Wrestling with deep questions leads to spiritual growth and sometimes changes our identity forever. Jacob's name became Israel ("God wrestler") to reflect his new identity (see Genesis 32:22–28).

Whenever we go through deep waters, we experience a season of suffering and questioning. We want life to make sense. John Maes says, "The relationship between meaning and suffering is of particular importance [when we try to help people]. No matter what the cost, a person will try to find meaning in suffering."[38]

Basic Resources for Christians

Christianity provides a rich understanding of the meaning of suffering and gives us faith resources like no other. Consider:

- The God of the Bible is a passionate and compassionate being. The person Jesus Christ is remembered for his suffering.
- The Bible is filled with believers who suffer and struggle with God.
- Early Christians felt it a privilege to suffer for their Lord.
- God's tender presence is everywhere—including, in the words of Psalm 23, "the valley of the shadow."

People may agree on central doctrines. They may worship and serve together in the work of the kingdom. But when faced with a crisis of disappointment, loss, grief, or pain, differences manifest. So what is going on?

It may very well have to do with the stages of faith development (or human development). Jim Fowler, Sam Keen, and Erik Erikson have described these so well in their books.[39] While I have borrowed from their ideas, I want to focus more narrowly here to describe faith as it relates to pain and suffering. I prefer to speak in terms of *levels* or *depths* of faith rather than stages. Think of believers diving down, deeper and deeper, as they let God take them into depths of release, peace, wisdom, obedience, and freedom.

Let's take a closer look at each of the levels. We'll begin with the following table, which gives you a quick outline of them. Then we'll unpack them one by one.

Levels of Faith in Times of Suffering

The following table provides a quick summary of six levels of faith and their attributes. We will take a closer look at them directly following.

FAITH DESCRIPTION	EXPECTATION	FAITH THEME
Simple Reliant Faith	God takes care of me	Trust
Moralistic Faith	God must be fair	Judgment
Adaptive Faith	God is telling me something	Learning
Complex Faith	Suffering builds character	Wisdom
Incarnational Faith	God suffers with me	Comfort/Paradox
Sacrificial Faith	God invites me to suffer with him on behalf of others	Purpose/Identity

Looking into the Depths of Faith

Faith can be described many different ways. Here we'll explore how the different levels of faith shape our responses to painful life experiences.

Simple Reliant Faith

This faith is nurtured every time a parent provides love and comfort to a child so that child feels safe. The core feature is trust, and the expected result is security. This is the foundation for all other levels of faith.

When danger or pain invades our lives, we ask questions like, "Why isn't God taking care of me?" "Has God forgotten me?" In Psalm 42, this dialogue shows up in two verses, ending on a note of trust.

> I say to God my Rock,
>> "Why have you forgotten me?
> Why must I go about mourning,
>> oppressed by the enemy?"
>>>> (Psalm 42:9)

> Why, my soul, are you downcast?
>> Why so disturbed within me?
> Put your hope in God,
>> for I will yet praise him,
>> my Savior and my God.
>>>> (Psalm 42:11)

Moralistic Faith

At this level, we expect life to be fair. When something goes wrong, we expect there is a good reason. We wonder what we have done wrong. Since God must be fair, we ask, "What did I do to deserve this?" After all, it was David who said, "I have never seen the righteous forsaken or their children begging bread" (Psalm 37:25).

Jesus decries the moralistic faith of some who explain disasters as only the result of someone's sin or moral impurity. This kind of faith was prominent among the Jews of his time, but Jesus says it is just not that simple.

> "Those eighteen who died when the tower in Siloam fell on them—do you think they were more guilty than all the others living in Jerusalem?" (Luke 13:4)

When his disciples ask why the man in John 10 was born blind, Jesus is blunt in contradicting them.

> His disciples asked him, "Rabbi, who sinned, this man or his parents, that he was born blind?" "Neither this man nor his parents sinned," said Jesus, "but this happened so that the works of God might be displayed in him." (John 9:2–3)

Adaptive Faith

In a more resilient faith, when suffering occurs, we look for something to come out of it. We wonder if God is showing us something important, and we strain to look ahead with an attitude of compliance. We are likely to ask, "What is God telling me to do, or to change in my life?"

The apostle Paul, for one, wrestled with a painful problem and concluded that God was teaching him a personal lesson.

> To keep me from becoming conceited [because of these surpassingly great revelations], I was given a thorn in my flesh, a messenger of Satan, to torment me. Three times I pleaded with the Lord to take it away from me. But he said to me, "My grace is sufficient for you, for my power is made perfect in weakness." Therefore I will boast all the more gladly about my weaknesses, so that Christ's power may rest on me. That is why, for Christ's sake, I delight in weaknesses, in insults, in hardships, in persecutions, in difficulties. For when I am weak, then I am strong. (2 Corinthians 12:7–10)

Pain can be more than a learning opportunity; it can be a blessing that moves one to self-examination and moral correction. Consider the prodigal son.

> When he came to himself he said, "How many of my father's hired hands have bread enough and to spare, but here I am dying of hunger! I will get up and go to my father, and I will say to him, 'Father, I have sinned against heaven and before you; I am no longer worthy to be called your son; treat me like one of your hired hands.'" (Luke 15:17–19 NRSV)

The prodigal son finds himself reduced to feeding pigs, a particularly humiliating form of suffering for any Jew. In his degradation and despair, wishing he could eat the bean pods he was feeding the pigs, he "came to himself." He saw the error of his ways and took responsibility for his past and his future.

Complex Faith

At this level we recognize that life is much too complex for a simple cause/effect explanation for our problems. We understand that we are immersed in a wide sea, the sea of humanity, and our lives are part of a vast panorama of human stories. We realize there are countless circumstances and forces in life that flow over and around each other like currents in the ocean. We yearn for greater understanding of why hardship or suffering has come upon us, but we are also ready to accept a deeper wisdom, a wider perspective, recognizing the mysterious nature of life. This is the faith the psalmist expresses in Psalm 66.

> For you, God, tested us;
>> you refined us like silver.
> You brought us into prison
>> and laid burdens on our backs.
> You let people ride over our heads;
>> we went through fire and water,
>> but you brought us to a place of abundance.
>
>   (vv. 10–12)

There is a bigger picture here. God is involved, and he "let people" do some terrible things that hurt others. In that same spirit, Joseph could look back many years later and see God's providence in spite of the wicked plans his brothers had carried out against him.

> Joseph said to them, "Don't be afraid. Am I in the place of God? You intended to harm me, but God intended it for good to accomplish what is now being done, the saving of many lives." (Genesis 50:19–20)

Instead of "Why me?" we may well say, "Why not me?" as Doug did earlier in this chapter. Recognizing our vulnerability can move us, in the words of philosopher Diogenes Allen, "off-center, and melt the illusion of our immense significance, to show us we are but dust and ashes."[40] Such humility is the beginning of wisdom, a wisdom that can ripen with patience into greater depth and compassion.

Incarnational Faith

As we move beyond the previous levels, we receive comfort from something beyond logic or reason. We recognize Jesus's presence through his cross. His words "I thirst" communicate a profound paradox: that the omnipotent God should be so diminished as to really know suffering and to suffer with us. We perceive the presence and compassion of God.

In answer to our question, "God, are you really there?" we are confronted, in Jesus's suffering and death, with him who entered our suffering to the depths.

> Surely he has borne our infirmities
> and carried our diseases;
> yet we accounted him stricken,
> struck down by God, and afflicted.
> But he was wounded for our transgressions,
> crushed for our iniquities;
> upon him was the punishment that made us whole,
> and by his bruises we are healed.
> (Isaiah 53:4–5 NRSV)

Sacrificial Faith

In the final level of faith, we seek to join Jesus in his suffering, letting pain lead us into a new sense of obedience and purpose. We are willing to let God use our suffering in the mysterious drama of his salvation story so that, in some way, others are blessed. This is an attitude of total acceptance, of surrender to let God use our lives however he chooses.

In this level of trust we enter into the life of God, letting God live through us. This is the faith that motivates one who is willing to suffer purposefully. Chapter 5 gave us glimpses of such people—those who have served by sharing another person's suffering willingly. When we follow Jesus and deliberately take the risk of pain or danger for someone else, we grasp a sense of God's higher purpose.

This calling shows up regularly in the New Testament. Paul wrote, "I want to know Christ—yes, to know the power of his resurrection and participation in his sufferings, becoming like him in his death" (Philippians 3:10).

The familiar call to "bear one another's burdens, and in this way . . . fulfill the law of Christ" (Galatians 6:2 NRSV) seems too simple, but lived to the fullest, it becomes our way of letting our lives be conformed to his image, living his way, fulfilling his law.

The Unifying Dynamic

In all these levels, the theme of trust is basic and actively being deepened through the exercise of faith. A believer is learning to let go of demands, to give up on explanations, and rather to dive deep into the love of God. The follower of the Crucified One grows to recognize that trusting God and seeking one's own comfort is but a shallow beginning. When we let the towering presence of the cross illuminate life, we start to see that compassion and grace are the keys to meaning. Our small and lonely selves are both comforted and inspired as we let ourselves expand to include the concerns of others. As we see life through the lens of God's suffering, God's love, and God's compassion, we become willing to trust him through anything. Letting go of our petty concerns, we dare to dive deeper into obedience—into situations where we do not know the outcome but trust that God's pattern is best.

I would be wrong if I have made this seem to be a well-traveled path we can expect to see regularly in ourselves and others. It should be clear by now that these levels and depths of faith do not occur for everyone. Many people stay in what Fowler calls a synthetic-conventional faith. They routinely accept the most common elements of their family and the institutions in which they have grown up, and they conform to the norms present there. But while ritual practices and communal fellowship provide comfort, hope, and meaning, they can cause us to miss out on the best God intends for us, the adventure of a deeper trust in him.

We don't leave levels behind. The trust foundation is the most important and is always involved in the adventure of going deeper. And at different times in life we are likely to move back and forth between the levels of faith. In a time of suffering, we may still cry out, "What is this all for?" when pain dominates our senses and overrules our trusting feelings.

The Aged Child in God's Embrace

Once I was visiting an old friend, a professor of weighty intellect, one who had lived the gospel and served decades in mission overseas. He was boundless in his passion to show us as students how to grasp the gospel so well we could share it with others freely.

But now he was in his last weeks with a painful cancer. During what turned out to be my last visit, he abruptly cried out, "Oh, God, what did I do to deserve this?" It was a question from the heart of a confused child, hidden away in the corner of an aged man.

Behind every mature face there may be a fearful child, a confused adolescent, a worried young adult, a bewildered middle-ager, perhaps a person of wisdom or a passion-filled disciple. In God's good providence they are all drawn together and embraced into himself.

As we let go more and more, our soul expands, and our identity is not lost but filled with a wonderful fullness that only comes from God. (See Ephesians 3:17–19).

Conclusion

The levels of faith I have identified are not intended to describe believers at different ages but, rather, their current levels of experience of God regardless of age. Recognizing these levels can help us make sense of what is going on in and around others and ourselves. The faith levels are not completely separated but function more like transparent overlays that add depth and richness of detail to our experience of faith. At any given time, a person may have one, some, or all levels of faith active or dormant. As caregivers, we honor people and their faith as we observe God at work in them; without tugging or pushing, we lovingly encourage each person to reach out and let God grasp them more fully as they dive into the depths with him.

FOR DISCUSSION OR PERSONAL REFLECTION

1 Which of the stories in this chapter is most memorable for you? Why is that?

2 Have you ever known someone in great pain or trouble who seemed to grow deeper in their faith? What happened? Have you ever seen someone go the opposite way?

3 If you can see one or more of the levels of faith in yourself, which ones are they?

4 What is one thing that seriously affected your own journey of faith?

CHAPTER 8

My Personal Journey toward Wholeness

WHEN I FIRST BEGAN WORKING ON THIS BOOK, I HAD A VIGOROUS, healthy mind and body. All my learning about acute suffering had come from my experiences as a pastor and researcher, from purposeful interviews, written testimonies, books, and other literature.

But more recently, God has allowed me some personal lessons in suffering. Suddenly I found myself in the story. And that is where I am today.

❤

In 2017, some routine tests showed that I had an aggressive form of prostate cancer, not the kind to just "watch and wait." At first I assumed it could be quickly removed with surgery, and I'd be done with it. But the doctors said that was not advisable. Instead they prescribed a long series of forty-four radiation treatments, every weekday for nine weeks, plus two years of hormone therapy.

When I asked the oncologist about my prognosis, he answered, "If you are not treated, you will be dead in two years. If you are treated, you have a 50 percent chance of being completely cured." Neither of these calculations was very comforting. I went home with those words echoing through my mind. I realized my life could be very limited. My "pride of life" was put out to pasture, irrelevant and stupid.

My doctor explained that follow-up monitoring methods are imprecise for this cancer, and it would take three to five years to get a clear idea of the success of my treatment. He said, "You will have to get used to living with uncertainty the rest of your life."

After a couple weeks of depression, I began to be buoyed up by the prayers of two special circles of friends that surrounded me. And I was humbled by the people of my church responding to my need for support. They gave me practical help with some of our home projects that I no longer had the strength to accomplish. Several people also took turns to drive me the forty-five miles each way for daily treatments. One neighbor I hardly knew insisted on driving me once a week because someone had done that for her the year before. It felt odd to me to be served so sacrificially. But slowly the love that these acts expressed embraced my heart in a way I had never experienced before.

By the middle of the treatment series, I was beginning to feel the weakness and decline in vigor the doctors had predicted. I could no longer say, "It hasn't affected me much." I tired easily and often fell asleep in the car regardless of who was driving. I could only work three or four hours a day in my office.

But my cancer had led to connections with people I hardly knew and to deeper relations with others. In the end, it is our relationships that save us. Relationships with brothers and sisters in faith who dare to connect with us and reaffirm that we belong to one another. These relationships confirmed my relationship with God, who gives us his ultimate promise, "I will never leave you or forsake you" (Hebrews 13:5 NRSV).

I came to realize that we all live with uncertainty, but I, like most others, had chosen to ignore that and live with the illusion that I am in control of my life. M. Scott Peck famously began his book *The Road Less Traveled* with the words "Life is difficult."[41] I was coming to realize that my life would include challenges I can only cope with either by great exertion or by greater acceptance of the help of others and the grace of God shown therein.

No longer could I escape the uncertainty of life. But I was learning to trust God and make different kinds of plans for different possibilities, both good and less than good. I've had to accept that at any time my health might swiftly head down the slope. My time might be very short. But I need to live all I can while I can, finish the most important projects I feel called to do, and ignore the rest. I read John 9:4 with a personal application: "We must work quickly to carry out the tasks assigned us by the one who sent us. The night is coming, and then no one can work" (John 9:4 NLT).

Shortly after my diagnosis I took a three-day solo retreat at a place where I could meditate without interruption and also receive some spiritual direction. During that visit I was encouraged to simply meditate on Jesus crucified. That led me to focus on how Jesus in his suffering and pain has already lived all my pain, uncertainty, or doubt. He experienced giving up control of his very body to strangers. In his agony he gave himself completely over, trusting to be held by his Father.

So my suffering has affected my faith by moving me from theoretical trust to visceral trust. God has taught me to give up control, to take orders from doctors and others. To prayerfully accept uncertainty.

My condition has taught me to appreciate every day more fully. My heart is moved by the wonder of the sunshine on our lake. The beauty of my wife's smile and the depth of her love. The affectionate embrace of a son or daughter. The sweetness and simplicity of a grandchild's trust. I am a little more emotional than before but not ashamed, not embarrassed.

These are some of my lessons. I can no longer handle the topic of this book clinically, if I ever did, standing apart. And that too is a good thing.

For Discussion or Personal Reflection

1 How has your own experience of troubled times shaped your view of life?

2 What have you learned about yourself from the way the author told his own story?

The Conclusion God Is Making

THE CROSS IS A STATEMENT OF GOD'S RADICAL CHOICE. SINCE God's creatures are bound to suffer, the Creator in solidarity with us has chosen to live in the same world. God made the world good. But he knew that humankind could tear the delicate lace of goodness. God takes the risk of being blamed for the results. Knowing the awful possibilities, the Lord of history was prepared to bear responsibility.

Perhaps God saw no other way to bring his sons and daughters to freedom and maturity. The awful price was foreseen, that the Lamb was slain "from the foundation of the world" (Revelation 13:8; cf. 1 Peter 1:20 NRSV).

Perhaps God could never forgive himself, or be forgiven by us, for creating a world of such awful possibilities if the Creator had not also chosen to inhabit that world with us. So the Divine One made an eternal choice to be incarnated into flesh, into pain, into bloody love, as a pact with suffering humankind. "God was reconciling the world to himself in Christ" (2 Corinthians 5:19).

In the cross of Christ, we find God's paradoxical answer to our suffering. Meditating on the cross of Jesus, we may sense Christ's presence and comfort. "Surely he took up our pain and bore our suffering. . . . He was pierced for our transgressions, he was crushed for our iniquities. . . . by his wounds are we healed" (Isaiah 53:4–5).

We are astonished into silence. There are no arguments left when we look into the eyes of the Crucified One.

When we perform simple acts of mercy for someone who is sick, or in prison, or naked, or hungry, Jesus says we will meet him (Matthew 25:40). Mother Teresa believed everyone has "the opportunity with us to do works of love . . . the opportunity with us to share the joy of loving and come to realize Gods presence."[42] Beyond the sighing requiem of the human spirit we begin to hear the notes of joy revealed in the cross and the resurrection.

The full text of Reinhold Niebuhr's prayer is seldom quoted.[43] It conveys the complete thought which we need to believe and to pray in order to live the life of faith to its fullest.

> God, grant me serenity to accept the things I cannot change, courage to change the things I can, and wisdom to know the difference; living one day at a time, enjoying one moment at a time; accepting hardship as a pathway to peace; taking, as Jesus did, this sinful world as it is, not as I would have it; trusting that You will make all things right if I surrender to Your will; so that I may be reasonably happy in this life and supremely happy with You forever in the next. Amen.

RESOURCES

Listening and Attending Skills

Listening well is your most powerful tool for connecting with people of all ages and conditions. When you listen well, the person you are listening to will know you care. And you will learn what is really important to them and what they may need.

When visiting someone who is isolated, hospitalized, or in some kind of trouble, you may want to "cheer them up" by talking about other things, or give advice to help them solve their problems. Resist the urge. None of it will do any good unless you have first listened a long time, so that you really understand what is going on in that person's life.

You may be tempted to talk about yourself and experiences you have that seem similar to theirs. Again, this will distract and keep you from learning what is really important to the person.

Think **ART**:

Ask questions to show you are interested. Always reflect to the other person what you hear—the facts and the feelings.

Resist the temptation to talk about yourself or give advice. Respond by talking about what you heard.

Take time to hear the person's *true feelings*. Those tell you what really matters. Every person's story is important.

The tools and exercises that follow will help, beginning with "Elements of Good Listening." Active, effective listening is hard work at first. Paying attention to every detail and withholding your own thoughts will pay off. Avoid thinking about what you will need to say next—if you ask good questions, you will not need to say much at all.

In "Identifying Emotions" dozens more words could be added to the list of positive and negative, worrisome or exciting feelings. Putting emotions into words may help a person identify his or her feelings for the first time; attaching names to inner feelings can open people up to further productive thinking and decision making.

Clearing up a detail is important sometimes, but it is much more valuable to identify the feelings involved. Then that person will know you understand.

The practice exercises on the following pages will help you check up on yourself and sharpen your listening skills. This can be fun, and it can improve your relationships at home too!

Also, for those occasions when someone needs help solving a personal problem, consider using the GROW coaching process shown in appendix C. It's invaluable when you are trying to help someone who has become dependent on you or expects too much of you, and you need to reaffirm your healthy boundaries.

Elements of Good Listening

Energy	Good listeners put a lot of energy into paying attention to the speaker. Quality listening is hard work.
Main ideas	Look for the main idea or feeling rather than details that may be interesting but irrelevant. Find what is really important to the speaker rather than yourself.
Emotions	Look for feelings that lie below the surface of words, and reflect these to the speaker. This is a key to the speaker's learning that he is really understood.

Voice	Listen for the tone and inflection that give clues to the inner seriousness, level of depth, honesty, or emotion of the speaker.
Respect	Good listeners show respect for the speaker, even when they do not agree with or understand what is being said.
Withhold judgment	Avoid judging. Accept individuals as they are and what they feel.
Eye contact	Look directly at the person to keep in touch and affirm that you want to understand, even when comments are confusing or murky.
Avoid reaction	Know your own areas of sensitivity or associations from past experience. Avoid responding out of your own emotional reactions.
Distractions	Listen for the *person*. Avoid thinking of physical features, dress, age, and other secondary details. Fight distractions from outside such as noise.
Time	We listen faster than we speak. You have time to think and listen carefully for the important words. Avoid premeditating what you might say in reply.
Get off yourself	Avoid thinking of how you look or sound. Put the speaker at the center.
Reflect	Repeat what you hear in summary, and interpret the emotions: "I heard you say . . ." "It sounds as if you are feeling . . ."
Check yourself	Ask if your comments are correct. This will confirm whether you are understanding or not, and the speaker will want to tell you more.
Habits	Exercise your skills regularly. Practice good listening habits wherever you are to establish the habit of paying attention.

Identifying Emotions

Feelings are important. Our emotions literally affect our bodies. Our heartbeat slows or quickens; we breathe rapidly or slowly, deeply or shallowly. Learning to talk about feelings is often a key to resolving our problems and going on to a healthier, happier life.

How do we know when we're in touch with our feelings? We use feeling words to describe our inner experiences. Here are some feeling words that describe common emotions. There are many more words we could use as well; these are just a sampler.

When we help people put a name to something they are feeling, frequently it enables them to move forward in thinking more clearly about their concerns.

excited	secure	uneasy	fearful
joyful	confident	vigilant	hopeless
delighted	bored	cautious	sorrowful
glad	hopeful	jealous	painful
silly	relaxed	uncertain	uncomfortable
playful	content	weary	anxious
amused	capable	worthless	angry
energetic	creative	stupid	rejected
sensuous	eager	skeptical	helpless
daring	relieved	uncertain	depressed
lonely	sorry	frustrated	embarrassed

Listening Exercises

Ask a friend or family member to help you practice the following listening exercises. Explain that the goal is for you to listen carefully and respond accurately, reflecting the speaker's meaning.

Listening Exercise 1

1. Ask the talker to tell about a problem situation they have encountered.

2. Your task is to respond in the following ways:

    A. Ask for more **information**. Examples:
    "Tell me more about how that happened."
    "What happened next?"
    "How did you take care of that?"

    B. Reflect the **feeling** level, the emotions the person may have experienced.
    "It sounds like that would be embarrassing (frustrating, painful, confusing, etc.)

    C. **Summarize** the event briefly, and how it affected the talker.
    Ask, *"Is that right?"*
    If not, *"Tell me more about it."*
    Always check to see if you understood correctly.

    D. **Do not** give advice to solve the problem. **Do not** compare by talking about something that happened to you.

3. Continue the process until both of you feel the incident is well understood. Then ask the talker how well you listened. Reflect on the experience together, then do another topic.

4. If you recruit two people to help you, ask the third person to observe without speaking at all. After finishing, ask your observer to tell you what they saw. Then switch the observer and talker so that each takes the other's place while you remain the listener.

Listening Exercise 2

Practice your listening skills informally with anyone—a family member, a child coming home from school, a coworker, anyone you meet. Don't mention that you are practicing your listening. Just be a friend.

❏ Ask how things have gone today. Reflect what you hear, and try to identify the person's feelings embedded in the things they tell you.

❏ Ask a friend to tell you about a hobby or passion they have. Again, reflect what you hear and identify feelings.

Conversation Starters

If you feel uncomfortable starting a conversation with someone you do not know, here are some suggestions. Good questions help a conversation take off.

❏ **Introduce yourself:** Hi! I'm (Your Name). I'm part of our church's care team (or whomever you represent). We have been concerned about you, so I came by to see how you are.

❏ **Ask open-ended questions.**
How are things going for you *today?*
Tell me about your family.
What do you enjoy doing when you feel well?
What's giving you trouble right now?
How is this affecting your relationship with God?

❏ **Follow up** with active listening and responding. You will learn a lot.

❏ **Ask permission** to read and pray.
Would you like me to read some Scripture today?
Would you like me to pray with you today?
Are there any special things you would like me to pray about?

❏ **Leave:** Is there anything I can take care of for you today, or someone you would like me to contact?

Mutual Giving and Receiving

Pick different people with whom to try one or more of the following approaches for creating an experience of giving and receiving.

Life Stories

Think of someone who has lived a lot of years or has been through some trying experiences. Arrange a visit someplace where it's easy to talk, maybe at a coffee shop. Ask him or her to share their experiences with you. *"I know you've been through a lot. I would appreciate it if you could tell me about it."*

Life Lessons

If you already know the person's story, you can start with something like this question: *"I'm wondering what you have learned about life that I might not know. Would you share something like that with me?"* (You can also ask this question directly after you've heard the person's story.)

Experienced Insight

Identify someone with life experience, tell them about a problem you have, and ask them to help you think it through. *"I'm wondering, what do you think is going on? Maybe you can help me figure out my options."* Do *not* ask, "What would you do?" That puts the person in the spot of feeling responsible if you follow their advice and get a bad result.

Practical Help

Ask for helpful information—for example: *"What have you learned about investing for retirement?"* Or *"Can you show me how to cook spinach so it's more fun to eat?"* Or *"Do you understand how a carburetor on a lawn mower works?"* Something the person might know and you would like to know.

When you have finished one or more of the above exercises, ask yourself how you think the conversation affected the person you were talking with. If it seems appropriate, explain to them that you are trying to learn more about strengthening relationships, and thank them for the conversation. See how that person lights up, knowing that he or she has helped you.

Healthy Boundaries and Personal Coaching

Checklist to Test Your Boundaries

DRS. JOHN TOWNSEND AND HENRY CLOUD, AUTHORS OF THE groundbreaking book *Boundaries*, provide an abundance of information to help us manage our boundaries effectively.[44] Drawing on its wisdom and my own experience as a caregiver and pastor, I've developed the following checklist. If we find ourselves doing something for someone when we don't want to, we need to consider which of the following unhealthy reasons may be driving us, and then change that picture.

❏ We enjoy being a rescuer; it makes us feel good about ourselves.

❏ We enjoy parenting someone who needs rescuing or continual help.

❏ We are afraid to disappoint that person because he or she will feel pain.

❏ We are afraid they will be angry or do something to make us feel guilty.

❏ We are burdened with feelings of guilt (not necessarily *real* guilt).

❏ We believe God intends us to help others with no limits.

❏ We believe we are the only one who can help.

What to Do When You Are Becoming Overextended

1. Have a support group, whether formal or informal—two or more family members, friends, or other people you trust and who understand what you are trying to do.

2. Prepare yourself for the situation. Practice saying no in a safe place with your group. Pray for guidance from God, with 2 Corinthians 9:7 or other Scripture in mind. Clarify your boundaries in your mind. We can keep good boundaries in place when we have a spiritual emotional home in God and with others who give us security, affirmation, and love.

3. When talking with the person you are serving, respond with empathy, reflecting the person's feelings. "I see that this situation is hard for you. It makes you feel afraid, (distressed, uncertain, confused, etc.)."

4. Assert your boundaries (limits). Don't explain in detail why you cannot do what the persons wants. Just say something like, "There's only so much I can do. I'm sorry, but you need to find a different way to take care of this problem. Maybe you can call Love INC or someone else who can help."

5. Consider shifting the conversation into a coaching mode if you feel you can make a difference this way. Help the person develop a plan for action that they can carry out without your involvement. You may find the next section on the GROW coaching process useful.

GROW: Coaching toward Practical Choices and Autonomy

The **GROW** model (Goal/Realities/Options/What, When) was developed in the 1980s by business coaches Graham Alexander, Alan Fine, and Sir John Whitmore. Use this process to help another person develop a plan of action that does not include you to make it work. It can be applied in many situations—your family, your business, your profession, or elsewhere. It is crucial that the person you are coaching develops and verbalizes their own answers to the questions.

Goal. What is the main thing that needs to be accomplished? What is the important goal today? Focus on one thing that is most essential to help the person. Whatever it is, find out and name it.

> *Examples:* Pay the rent. Get a job. Wash clothes. Take my medicine on time. Manage the kids. Resolve a strained relationship. Write a letter to my parent.

Realities. What are the main realities involved—resources that might help, the facts of the matter, who else is involved, the complicating factors, urgency, and other details.

> *Examples:* Need by end of month. Don't have transportation. I have friends who can help. Husband gets angry-drunk. Teacher sent note requesting meeting. Who can help? Need childcare so I can get to work.

Options. What are all the different things you could do to address this? In this step it is crucial that the person generate all sorts of choices and stimulating ideas from their own mind. Avoid thinking for them.

> *Examples:* Rent a washer instead of buy. Call teacher to make appointment. Apply for work at places I can walk to. Take Dial-A-Ride. Ask sister for money to help. Call husband's brother for help. Get fresh clothes from Goodwill store. Call Love INC for referral.

Probe repeatedly: "What else can you possibly do?" "Is there some crazy idea you might think of?" "What do you think someone else might do?" You will be tempted to offer your own ideas, but again, don't. The individual may believe your idea is always best, and this will prevent their adopting their own idea and acting on it.

What, When. Which option will you choose? What do you want to do? Which option will help the most?

This is a critical moment. The person must decide. Avoid prompting them.

Once they've decided, the next question is, When will you do it? Fixing a time and date is vital to get the plan moving. If two or three steps have been identified, ask which should be done first, which next, and so on.

———— 💜 ————

Wrap up the conversation by summarizing the whole matter. What is the main goal, which action has been chosen, and when will the person do it? Compliment the person for thinking of these ideas. Encourage them with words of affirmation such as "I know you can do this."

Nurturing the Caregiver

Caregivers get worn down. Listening with compassion to the experiences people share can be exhilarating, but it can also be draining. Hearing about things that are discouraging, or even tragic, and knowing you cannot do a thing to change it, can be depressing. Listening, caring, and helping are hard work.

We get tired. We get worn out.

In chapter 5, in the section "Maintaining Healthy Boundaries," I mentioned some cautions and guidelines for keeping your balance as a caregiver, especially when facing difficult relationships and situations. Let's look more closely at some ways you can maintain your own health and nurture yourself so you can continue as a productive caregiver.

Peer Group or Support Group

Going it alone is not a good idea. You need to meet regularly with a group of other caregivers or with people who understand well what you are engaged in. At these gatherings, perhaps monthly, you can review how things are going in your helping relationships. You can celebrate the good things you have seen, safely share your concerns about tough situations and difficult people, and talk without hesitation about feeling inadequate or confused about what you should do. As others also share their experiences, all of you can gain practical insights and courage from one another.

Pastoral Support

You need a good relationship with your pastor or spiritual director, with whom you can raise questions about spiritual matters. Sometimes a person you are helping may ask, "What does the Bible say about _____?" or they may request input on spiritual decisions. When you do not feel comfortable or competent to give an answer, you need to be able to say, "I will find out more about that for you," knowing that you have a resource you can turn to. And on occasions when you feel inadequate for the task of caregiving or feel guilty that you cannot do what someone wants or expects from you. Your pastor or spiritual director can help you resolve those personal issues.

Family and Friends

Don't neglect your network of family and friends. They are a big part of the fabric that holds your life together. They will help you feel normal and happy at times when you are worn down. And they deserve your love and attention just as much as anyone you are serving as a caregiver. So take time for your family and friends.

But keep your caregiving relationships confidential; do not share personal details with your family. And if your family has its own issues and is troubled, don't take your caregiving as an excuse to get away and avoid working on those issues. You will be stronger and happier if all the parts of your life are intact and healthy.

Spiritual Practices

Keep a regular pattern of prayer and Bible reading. Journaling as a part of your devotional habits is another way to enhance the freshness of your prayer time. When your own spiritual life keeps you engaged in conversation with God, you are better equipped to be a spiritual help to others. Your successes are not yours alone; they are the Lord's, who is working through you. And what seems like a setback or a failure is not solely yours, either. Each event needs to be seen through the lens of God's grace in your life.

Remember to pray for individuals you have chosen to visit or help. Stop and pray for a few moments before going in to see someone at the hospital or wherever that person may be.

Supervision

You need to be accountable to someone, whether it's your peer group, a care team leader, or your pastor. Again, it's important that you not try to function as a lone ranger. We all have weaknesses and blind spots, and a supervisor who helps you recognize and remedy those problems is a huge asset. They can safeguard you from making mistakes or accepting unrecognized and unrealistic risks.

Vulnerability

Nurturing vulnerable people makes you yourself more vulnerable. Be very self-aware of your own weaknesses and temptations. Elder abuse and sexual abuse are all too common, and they frequently grow out of a relationship that was originally benign and supportive. Moreover, each of us is liable at times to be driven by fear of failure or by guilt over something we think we should have done differently. At the risk of overemphasizing the point, a peer group, pastor, or supervisor is essential to turn to for reflection and help.

Communicating Feelings and Needs

Be upfront and honest when you face a challenge to your boundaries. Communicate your needs and emotions lovingly and honestly. For instance, if you face an intractable person, you can say, "I love you, but I need you to know that when you (name the behavior), I feel hurt and frustrated. If you choose to take care of _____, then I will feel better about working with you. But if you choose not to change that, I cannot help you any further. Perhaps there is someone else who can work with you."

This is only an example, but the key elements are: (1) affirming that you care and/or love the person; (2) saying clearly how a particular behavior of theirs affects you; (3) expressing your hope they will change and you can continue in the relationship; and (4) stating that if the person chooses not to change their action/attitude, they will need to find someone else to help them.

Continuing Education

Peer groups often include some form of ongoing education—perhaps a book discussion or a study provided by your pastoral care leader. If not, look for opportunities and resources yourself. The more we work with people in need, the more we realize what there is to learn about how to help both them and ourselves in the challenges of life.

Boundaries, Boundaries

You are responsible for yourself; others are responsible for themselves. We reach across and help one another. Our love for one another pulls us across boundaries to assist, to support, and to give affection or encouragement. But you and I cannot make someone else happy, and we must continually remember that our happiness should not be held hostage to someone else's grief, anger, anxiety, disappointment, or judgment of us. This is a difficult spiritual principle to maintain, and it will be challenged again and again. So we must pay all the more attention to maintaining our own healthy boundaries. Then we can also be most effective as caregivers.

Acknowledgments

I CANNOT POSSIBLY NAME EVERYONE WHO CONTRIBUTED TO MAKing this book a reality. The following are just some whose help has been invaluable.

My friend and colleague, Dr. Stanley A. Rock, more than anyone else was the sparkplug that fired my confidence and courage as a researcher and writer. The people of Saranac Community Church provided generous sabbatical time which laid the early foundation for this study.

Barry Matthews invested his finest efforts in improving my writing. Roger Grandia gave me invaluable suggestions that shaped the structure of this book. Several friends and colleagues read and helped make this a better work, among them Craig and Kathy Smith, Keith Foisy, Marcia Weeks, Bob Braman, and Tom Woudstra.

I am exceedingly grateful to the dozens of people who told me their stories, in some cases revisiting painful scenes and precious losses. Without their generous sharing, there would be no book. In addition, there were dozens who studied the material in class, raised good questions, and field tested my ideas. My friend Sherwin Weener has been a great source of encouragement through all the years I have worked on this project.

This book would not have been published without the experience, wisdom, and energy my publisher, Kevin Miles, gave to this project. Our editor, Bob Hartig, improved the expression of my ideas so well; I felt he really understood my mind and became my writing partner. I cannot thank these two gentlemen enough.

No statement of gratitude could be sufficient to thank my wife, Mary Ann, for her consistent support and encouragement. She read and improved my writing, challenged and clarified my thinking, suggested improvements, and in every way was my faithful cheerleader the whole time.

Notes

CHAPTER 2: Crossing into Alien Territory

1. Mike Yankoski, *Under the Overpass: A Journey of Faith on the Streets of America* (Colorado Springs: Multnomah, 2005), 78–79.

2. Tony Campolo, address given in 2003 at The Feast, an Evangelical Covenant Church conference in Colorado.

3. Mother Teresa, *A Gift for God: Prayers and Meditations* (New York: Harper & Row, 1975), 69.

4. Arthur C. McGill, *Suffering: A Test of Theological Method* (Philadelphia: Westminster, 1982), 95, 114.

5. Mary Bosanquet, *The Life and Death of Dietrich Bonhoeffer* (New York: Harper & Row, 1968), 217.

6. Michael Westmoreland-White, Glen Stassen, and David P. Gushee, "Disciples of the Incarnation," *Sojourners* 23, no. 4 (May 1994), 26.

CHAPTER 3: Simple Gifts Make the Difference

7. When Richard died some years later, I had responsibility for disposing of his hundreds of books. Among them were a few volumes on literary criticism. I was uncertain what to do with them. But I had become acquainted with our daughter's high school English teacher, who was an excellent educator. She had a great impact on our daughter, who with this teacher's guidance was gaining skill and confidence in creative writing. So I visited the teacher and brought a few of Richard's literary criticism books along to see if she would like to have any of them. When she opened the first one she saw Richard's name inside. With some emotion, she asked me, "Did these books really belong to Richard ———?" Her question conveyed awe, as if he were a famous person. I assured her it was the same Richard. She told me she had taken his classes in creative

writing at the university during his postgraduate years. She said, "He was the best teacher I have ever had!" Her words showed how much was lost in Richard's short and frustrated life, but also how his gifts still affected and blessed an unknown number in the next generation.

8. From lectures by Carl Nieswonger at Town and Country pastors' event, Michigan State University, 1969; and from Elisabeth Kubler-Ross, *On Death and Dying: What the Dying Have to Teach Doctors, Nurses, Clergy, and Their Own Families* (New York: Scribner, 1969), 173–79.

9. Atul Gawande, *Being Mortal: Medicine and What Matters in the End* (New York: Henry Holt, 2014), 5.

10. Gawande, *Being Mortal*, 155.

11. Striking testimonies from hospice care and counsel can be found in Maggie Callanan and Patricia Kelley, *Final Gifts: Understanding the Special Awareness, Needs, and Communications of the Dying* (New York: Bantam, 1993).

12. Joseph's House is a faith-based nonprofit organization started by members of the ecumenical Church of the Saviour in 1990. At the time of my interviews there, Joseph's House admitted only homeless men dying of AIDS, but they began to welcome women and people dying of cancer in 2006. However, AIDS patients are still given priority in admission.

CHAPTER 4: The Blessings Go Both Ways

13. Erika Schuchardt, *Why Is This Happening to Me?: Guidance and Hope for Those Who Suffer* (Minneapolis: Augsburg, 1989), 103.

14. Charles Garfield and Cindy Spring, *AIDS Caregiving* cassette tape (The Charles Garfield Group, 1993).

15. Mother Teresa, *A Gift for God: Prayers and Meditations* (New York: Harper & Row, 1975), 27.

16. Malcolm Muggeridge, *Something Beautiful for God: Mother Teresa of Calcutta* (San Francisco: Harper & Row, 1971), 41.

17. John Powell, *Unconditional Love: Love without Limits* (Naperville, IL: Argus, 1978).

18. In her book *Why Is This Happening to Me?: Guidance and Hope for Those Who Suffer* (Minneapolis: Augsburg, 1989), Erika Schuchardt recounts a disabled woman's tale of frustration and disappointment. Luise Habel had good experiences as a young woman in the Protestant Youth Group, even though she was always in a wheelchair. As an adult, she had been an

office worker. She contacted her regional youth pastor to discuss training as a professional parish worker. His reaction seemed encouraging: she would be notified when the next training courses were scheduled. Months later she learned that the training had already been offered and she had not been notified because the pastor and others thought her handicap was too much after all.

19. David G. Myers, *The Pursuit of Happiness: Who Is Happy, and Why?* (New York: Avon Books, 1992).

20. Ralph McGill, *Suffering, A Test of Theological Method* (Philadelphia: Westminster, 1982), 76.

21. McGill, *Suffering*, 75, 77. For more on this subject, consider these passages from Scripture:

> "Very truly, I tell you, the Son can do nothing on his own, but only what he sees the Father doing; for whatever the Father does, the Son does likewise. The Father loves the Son and shows him all that he himself is doing." (John 5:19–20 NRSV)

The Holy Spirit is also doing things which bring glory to Christ and accomplish the Father's purposes, not some agenda of His own.

> "When the Spirit of truth comes, he will guide you into all the truth; for he will not speak on his own, but will speak whatever he hears, and he will declare to you the things that are to come. He will glorify me, because he will take what is mine and declare it to you." (John 16:13–14 NRSV).

22. Paul Fiddes, in *The Creative Suffering of God* ([Oxford: Oxford University Press, 1988], 123), expands this thought eloquently: "When we ask, 'Who is God?' we are confronted by an event which we can only describe in relational terms: we speak of a son relating to a Father in suffering and love. There is a son crying out to a Father whom he has lost ('My God, why have you forsaken me?') and so there is implied a Father who suffers the loss of a son. . . . At the same time as they are most separated they are most one, for they are united in loving purpose . . . and the Spirit of love is between them." Fiddes credits Karl Barth with the seminal idea he expresses in this paragraph.

CHAPTER 5: Shared Suffering and Bonds of Healing Love

23. This insight is not new, but in this situation it was revolutionary.
In creating Hull House, Jane Addams clearly wanted it to be a place where young women from secure and privileged families could engage

poverty-stricken people on a daily basis, working and learning together so that not only were the needy helped but the young women gained a deeper perspective and purpose in living. "Addams saw Hull House not only as a place to help the poor; it was a place where the affluent could surrender to an ennobling vocation." David Brooks, *The Road to Character* (New York: Random House, 2015), 32–33.

24. Louis Evely, *Suffering* (Garden City, NY: Doubleday, 1974), 25.

25. Paul Fiddes, *The Creative Suffering of God* (Oxford: Oxford University Press, 1988),173. The whole theology of salvation has also been described in terms of intimacy by Dick Westley, *Redemptive Intimacy: A New Perspective for the Journey to Adult Faith* (Mystic, CT: Twenty-Third Publications, 1981).

26. Fiddes, *Creative Suffering of God*, 16.

27. Howard Clinebell and Charlotte Clinebell, *The Intimate Marriage* (New York: HarperCollins, 1970), 43–45.

28. Erika Schuchardt, *Why Is This Happening to Me?: Guidance and Hope for Those Who Suffer* (Minneapolis: Augsburg, 1989), 136, 110.

29. John L. Maes, *Suffering: A Caregiver's Guide* (Nashville: Abingdon, 1990), 153–4. His footnote included in this quote refers to M. Imara, "Dying as the Last Stage of Growth," in *Death: The Final Stage of Growth*, Elizabeth Kűbler-Ross, ed. (Englewood Cliffs, NJ: Prentice Hall, 1975).

CHAPTER 6: Discovering Jesus's Presence

30. The line "Bruised, divided, full of pain" is quoted from Mother Teresa, *The Joy in Loving* (New York: Penguin, 2000), 347. Richard A. Jansma, the author of "Bloodsweat," sometimes used the pen name R.A.J. Conry.

31. Elizabeth Elliot, in an address at the First Church of the Nazarene in Pasadena, CA, broadcast on *Focus on the Family* radio, 1990. A similar idea is implied in her book, *A Path through Suffering: Discovering the Relationship Between God's Mercy and Our Pain* (Grand Rapids: Revell, 1990).

32. Mother Teresa, *Words to Love By* (Notre Dame, IN: Ave Maria Press, 1983), 7.

33. Mother Teresa, *A Gift for God: Prayers and Meditations* (New York: Harper & Row, 1975), 77.

34. Malcolm Muggeridge, *Something Beautiful for God*, (San Francisco: Harper & Row, 1971), 37.

35. Mother Teresa, *Words to Love By*, 22.

36. Mother Teresa, *Words to Love By*, 79.

37. Dietrich Bonhoeffer, *Letters and Papers from Prison: The Enlarged Edition* (New York: Macmillan, 1971), 391.

CHAPTER 7: What Happens to Faith under Pressure

38. John L. Maes, *Suffering: A Caregiver's Guide* (Nashville: Abingdon, 1990), 23–24.

39. Jim Fowler and Sam Keen, *Life Maps: Conversations on the Journey of Faith* (Waco, Texas: Word Books, 1978), 42–100; Jim Fowler, *Stages of Faith: The Psychology of Human Development and the Quest for Meaning* (San Francisco: Harper & Row, 1981), 117–211; Erik Erikson, *Childhood and Society*, 2d ed. (New York: Norton, 1963), 247–73.

40. Diogenes Allen, *Traces of God* (Cambridge, MA: Cowley, 1981), 50.

CHAPTER 8: My Personal Journey toward Wholeness

41. M. Scott Peck, *The Road Less Traveled: A New Psychology of Love, Traditional Values, and Spiritual Growth* (New York: Simon & Schuster, 1978).

EPILOGUE: The Conclusion God Is Making

42. Mother Teresa, *Words to Love By* (Notre Dame, IN: Ave Maria Press, 1983), 35.

43. Reinhold Niebuhr first wrote this prayer for a sermon at Heath Evangelical Union Church in Heath, Massachusetts, but used it widely with some variations in sermons as early as 1934; and first published it in 1951 in a magazine column, as reported in Philip Zaleski and Carol Zaleski, *Prayer: A History* (Boston: Houghton Mifflin: 2005), 127.

APPENDIX C: Healthy Boundaries and Personal Coaching

44. For more on the nature and importance of healthy boundaries, see Henry Cloud and John Townsend, *Boundaries: When to Say Yes, How to Say No, to Take Control of Your Life*, rev. ed. (Grand Rapids: Zondervan, 2017).

CPSIA information can be obtained
at www.ICGtesting.com
Printed in the USA
FSHW012209221219
65088FS

9 780996 232845